"What's the matter, Carey?"
Gavin's words had an edge of concern she had never heard from him before.

Carey felt defensive and unsure of herself. "The reason I pulled away from you is something you'll never understand."

"Carey, you've shown up on my doorstep un-invited. You willingly returned my kisses. Now you say I'll never understand. What does it take to get the message through to you, Carey? I care about you! Don't waste yourself on someone you don't love. You'll regret it for a lifetime."

"How can you know about love or about me?" Carey challenged.

She spun around and ran down the steps toward her car. Gavin followed, catching her by the arm, pulling her up against him. She stared into his emotion-darkened eyes.

"Marry the old plant doctor, if that's what you want, Carey. But just remember, you had your chance at real love, and you ran away from it." Swiftly, he released her and disappeared inside his mansion.

Dear Reader,

The Promise Romance™ you are about to read is a special kind of romance written with you in mind. It combines the thrill of newfound romance and the inspiration of a shared faith. By combining the two, we offer you an alternative to promiscuity and superficial relationships. Now you can read a romantic novel—with the romance left intact.

Promise Romances™ will introduce you to exciting places and to men and women very much involved in today's fast-paced world, yet searching for romance and love with commitment—for the fulfillment of love's promise. You will enjoy sharing their experiences. Most of all you will be uplifted by a romance that involves much more than physical attraction.

Welcome to the world of Promise Romance™— a special kind of place with a special kind of love.

For the Love of Roses

Donna Winters

Promise Romances

Thomas Nelson Publishers • Nashville • Camden • New York

In memory of my father, Donald W. Rogers
small town florist
man of principle

Published in Nashville, Tennessee, by Thomas Nelson, Inc., and distributed in Canada by Lawson Falle, Ltd., Cambridge, Ontario.

Printed in the United States of America.

All of the characters and events in this book are fictitious. Any resemblance to actual persons, living or dead, or to actual events is purely coincidental.

ISBN 0-8407-7360-9

Chapter One

Wandering between the benches of potted plants, Carey McIlwain paused momentarily to caress the leaf of a budding poinsettia. Her face was pensive as she felt the texture of the leaf. She barely noted the morning sunlight as it filtered through the glass of the greenhouse her grandfather had built decades before. Carey's mind was full of the traumatic events of the past two weeks—events which, at age twenty-four, had left her in charge of the family florist business.

Her father, a well-known plant grower, and her mother, a respected floral designer, had been taken from her suddenly in an automobile accident. Returning to their home in Stockport from a concert twenty miles to the east in Rochester, Carey's parents were caught in a late October snow squall moving across Lake Ontario to upstate New York. Their car had slid off the expressway and crashed into a cement abutment.

Carey had received the devastating news at her apartment in Harrington. Hastily, she had packed a few belongings and left the comforting arms of her roommate and coworker at the elementary school where they taught to arrange for the funeral in Stockport. Marilee had brought the remainder of Carey's possessions to

Stockport and delivered her resignation to the principal of their school.

Carey's eyes watered as she thought of her parents' deaths, the music students she would never teach again, and the difficulties facing her in attempting to run the business. Although Carey had helped with the holiday rush during her high school years, she knew little of the nuts and bolts behind growing and wholesaling potted plants, or artistically arranging floral pieces. The loss of her parents and the demands of managing a business had sorely tested Carey's faith.

"Carey, there's a gentleman here who wants to see you," Maggie called to her from the back door of the retail shop, which opened into the first greenhouse.

"Be right there." Carey relied heavily on Maggie and Floyd Emery. They had worked with her parents for as long as she could remember.

Maggie helped out in the shop answering the phone, taking orders, doing the bookkeeping, and assisting with the corsages and centerpieces. Floyd handled the deliveries, some of the greenhouse work, and did general maintenance. Maggie and Floyd had assured her they would help in any way possible. Unfortunately, the business barely ran in the black, and unless profits improved, she might be forced to sell out.

The thought troubled her as she walked toward the front of the shop. Carey valued the tradition that had kept the business in her family and loathed the idea of giving it up. But her younger brother Todd, a graduate student at Cornell, expected to take over the reins as soon as he finished his degree. Could she handle managing the business without Todd's assistance for the next several months?

"Gavin Jack, Jack Brothers Roses." Carey looked into the deep-set eyes of the gruff-looking man who seemed

6

not to notice her extended hand. "I've just delivered the last of your rose orders. Unless I see some cash, your account is suspended. That's company policy."

Carey struggled to sound confident. "I had no idea our account was in arrears. I'll do everything possible to bring it up to date, but I have to have delivery next week."

Carey remembered Maggie's comment that several dozen roses had already been ordered for centerpieces for a large banquet at the local college. With roses included in the banquet theme, there was no possibility of substituting another cut flower. McIlwain Greenhouses *needed* the income from these orders to bolster its shaky finances.

Gavin Jack's expression remained unchanged. "Like I said—no cash, no roses."

A three-day stubble covering his face added to his already rough appearance. The upturned collar of his rope-trimmed, black leather jacket reminded her of a first-class hood, but Gavin Jack had to be thirty-five, at least. *A little old for the high-school hood image*, Carey mused.

But as intimidating as Gavin seemed, Carey was unexplainably attracted to the tall, broad-shouldered rose grower. There was a compelling look about his countenance, his angular jawline, and the strong set of his chin.

"Where's Pat?" His question stung Carey, sending pain deep into the pit of her stomach.

"My parents no longer run this operation. I do," she asserted, grasping for control.

She was unaware of the vulnerable expression crossing her features at the mention of her father's name. The teal-blue flecks in her bulky sweater enhanced her unusually deep-blue irises. Shoulder-length auburn hair, which was neither carefully curled nor perfectly straight, framed her face. Her rugged, stained jeans and pushed-up sleeves indicated she was not afraid of getting her hands dirty.

Gavin Jack ran a hand through his tousled, dark hair, then doffed his black leather knickerbocker cap. "I'll stop by on my way through next week, but if you don't have the payment, you don't get the roses." He turned on his heel and strode out the side door.

Carey watched as he backed out of the driveway in a brand-new white delivery van with "Jack Brothers Roses" emblazoned in red on the side. Jack Brothers looked like a prosperous operation.

"Why didn't you tell him about your parents?" Maggie gently asked, putting an arm around her shoulders like a comforting grandmother.

Carey brushed the back of her hand across her eyes, wiping away the tears. "I just couldn't. I've got to take responsibility for what happens from now on. I can't play on the sympathy of others to succeed."

"But surely under the circumstances…"

Carey hugged Maggie. "Under the circumstances, I think you'd better show me the books, so I'll know just what I'm up against."

Maggie and Carey sat down at the cluttered desk and went over the accounts item by item. When they were done, Carey had resolved the immediate problem. She determined not to draw a salary herself beyond what was necessary to meet her living expenses. The extra revenue would be used to pay off overdue accounts. Jack Brothers Roses was on the top of that list.

"You still haven't figured out how to pay for the funeral," Maggie mentioned, shoving aside the bulky ledger.

"I know. Dad wanted those expenses paid as soon as

possible, too. He even mentioned it in his will." She drew in a labored breath. "I'll just have to go see Mr. Flemming at the bank."

"Charlie Flemming is a very understanding man. You'll work it out." Maggie patted her hand.

Maggie was right. When Carey sat down with the portly Mr. Flemming an hour later, they were able to work out a payment plan Carey believed she would be able to meet.

Following lunch, she returned to the shop. Carey was surprised to see a number of young people milling around inside. A fellow in his late thirties, holding a full-bent pipe, made his way toward her. Carey tried to remember where she had seen the face before. The collar-length brown hair, which partially covered his ears, and the closely trimmed mustache and beard definitely looked familiar.

"Ms. McIlwain, I'm Alex Hensley. We met the other day." He dropped his pipe into the sagging patch pocket of his tweed jacket. Clear hazel eyes swept over her form as she tried to place the kind smile, which cracked tiny lines in his ruddy complexion.

Quickly it came back to her. Dr. Hensley, who taught at the local state university, had introduced himself to her at the funeral home. Maggie had mentioned earlier this morning that he would be bringing his botany class by for a tour of the greenhouses.

"Of course, Dr. Hensley."

"Alex. Please."

"Then you must call me Carey. Sorry if I've kept you waiting. Right this way." Carey led the group into the first greenhouse. About twenty-five college sophomores followed.

"The first bench holds cyclamen and the others, poinsettias. We take cuttings in the summer months,

9

from stock plants. Most of the poinsettias will be sold wholesale. We'll keep just enough to retail ourselves." Carey noticed Alex standing at the back of the group, his eyes rarely leaving her.

She took the class through to the cold house where the azaleas were stored, into the large greenhouse behind, and into the bubble where more poinsettias were growing. Alex pointed out plant varieties of particular interest to his class, such as the various green plants grown for hanging baskets. Carey was thankful for any additions to her own explanations, for she had barely reacquainted herself with the greenhouses since her parents' funeral.

"Join me for coffee, Carey?" Alex asked after seeing the last of his students out the front door of the shop.

"Thank you, but," Carey hesitated as she looked up into his kind eyes. "I'd better get back to work," she answered reluctantly.

Maggie watered display plants nearby. Without really looking at her, Carey sensed her admonishing expression.

"You mean you're going to break with tradition?" Alex asked, one bushy eyebrow slightly higher than the other.

"What tradition is that, Dr. Hensley?" Carey couldn't help grinning at his persuasive appeal.

"Not Dr. Hensley, Alex. Remember? Your parents *always* joined me for coffee after a tour."

A mild aching pulsed through her, and Carey wondered if she'd ever get over those painful responses at the mere mention of her parents. Her thoughts must have registered on her face because Alex's eyes immediately clouded with concern.

"In that case," Carey forced brightness into her voice, "I can't refuse."

10

Carey pulled the collar of her violet-trimmed, gray ski parka tightly around her neck as they walked toward the Village Kitchen, less than a block away. Alex offered his arm as he escorted her through the bitter November breeze. She remembered then that several months had passed since a gentleman had walked between her and the road.

They settled into a corner booth in the small, nearly deserted restaurant. Red and white gingham cloths covered the tables. Ruffled curtains of the same fabric were tied back at each window. The homey atmosphere, however, did little to soothe the dull pain of loneliness Carey had felt since the accident.

"You're living in your parents' home, I assume?"

Carey nodded. "For now, anyway. It's only two houses from the shop, and it's paid for. I'm hoping I'll be able to..." She stopped suddenly at the thought of having to sell the house just to keep the business operating.

"Perhaps you'd like to tour the college greenhouse sometime." Alex skillfully directed the conversation toward a different topic. "I'm experimenting with Heliconias, and you might enjoy some of the tropical plants the students have been nurturing. I don't teach Monday mornings. Wouldn't business be slow enough so you could get away for a couple of hours? I could pick you up at ten."

"That won't be necessary. I can meet you there." Carey sipped her coffee and pondered her lack of botanical knowledge. "You'll have to forgive my ignorance, though. In all honesty, I wouldn't know a Heliconia if I saw one. I really don't know very much about plants. I never thought I'd..." *End up in the florist business* went unspoken.

Carey dropped her eyes, took a deep breath, and began again. "You could probably teach me a lot. I'm determined to learn this business as quickly as possible. Just recognizing some of the less common plants, like those in your greenhouse at the college, would be a good start."

"I'm looking forward to Monday already," Alex said, his face lighting with a smile. The laugh lines at the corners of his mouth deepened, and Carey noted how they added character to Alex's features.

As he walked her back to the florist shop, Alex placed his hand over Carey's, which rested in the crook of his arm. To Carey, the gesture seemed perfectly natural. She couldn't explain why, but she felt very comfortable with Alex.

When they stood in front of the door, Alex squeezed her hand and looked deep into her eyes. "You'll be in my prayers, Carey," he murmured, then he held the door for her. It seemed fitting that Alex was a Christian, Carey thought, as she watched him walk toward his car.

Later that afternoon, Carey waited on a customer who purchased a helium balloon. She took two phone orders, then started helping Maggie with the cut flower orders. Carey tried to concentrate as Maggie taught her how to arrange floral pieces and wrap cut flower stems for corsages, but for some reason her mind kept drifting back to Gavin Jack.

Gavin. Who was this man? Why should Carey even waste time wondering about him? Perhaps Gavin Jack was in her thoughts because the contrast between him and a man like Alex Hensley was so striking. *No two men could be more different*, Carey thought. *The only thing God gave them in common was an interest in plants.*

Carey smiled at this thought, but then was reminded

that her own faith needed some renewing. Carey determined to make an effort to tear down the barriers she had erected between herself and God since the accident. She needed to return to Sunday school and church.

"Good night, Maggie. See you tomorrow," Carey called, as she double-checked the locked door from outside and turned toward home.

Carey's walk took her past the house her grandfather had built and occupied. The older, two-story shingled home belonged to someone else now, but Carey's aunt, uncle, and four of their seven children still lived a few miles away.

The third house from the shop was home to Carey. She had lived all of her life there until going off to college. It was a small ranch-style house, with three tiny bedrooms and a flagstone porch in front.

As Carey mounted the two front steps, she noticed a carton in front of the door. Puzzled, she unlocked the door and carried it inside. The cardboard flaps easily popped open, revealing a large fruit basket wrapped in yellow cellophane.

"How thoughtful," Carey half whispered to herself. "I wonder who…" She reached for the card stapled to the cellophane. It was a business card embossed with a shiny red rose in one corner. "Jack Brothers Roses" filled the center of the card.

Carey laid the card on the table and unwrapped the fruit. Of course, it was simply a business amenity, she reminded herself. For years, her parents had bought their roses from Jack Brothers, and probably her grandfather had too. Someone at Jack Brothers must have noticed the obituary and taken time to send the basket.

Carey removed two oranges, two bananas, and a small bunch of green grapes from the basket, and decided to share the rest with Maggie and Floyd. Carey picked up the card and laid it on the stack of cards sent with other gifts of flowers and food. So many had poured in since her parents' accident. Tonight, after supper, she would write more thank-you notes.

As Carey settled in front of her favorite Wednesday night TV show, she opened the drawer of her mother's antique cherry table and pulled out a pen and the thank-you cards. She picked the Jack Brothers business card off the stack and flipped it over. To her surprise, the back was covered with a hand printed message in tiny, neat, capital letters.

CAREY,
I WAS SHOCKED TO LEARN TODAY OF YOUR DOUBLE TRAGEDY. I EXTEND TO YOU AND YOUR BROTHER MY DEEPEST SYMPATHY. IF I CAN HELP YOU IN ANY WAY, PLEASE CALL ANY TIME, DAY OR NIGHT. G.J.

Carey was unsure how to react. Certainly, she would never have expected these sympathetic words from the steel-hard Gavin Jack, who had confronted her this morning over the unpaid bills. *A man like Gavin Jack must have an ulterior motive*, Carey thought. She read the note again and decided that must be it.

Swiftly, Carey penned an impersonal sentence on the preprinted card thanking Gavin for the fruit, then shoved it into an envelope and set it aside. She would prove to him one week from today that she neither needed, nor wanted, his consoling. She would pay him every penny she owed him when he delivered the roses next Wednesday morning.

14

Monday morning Carey awoke more refreshed than at any time since moving back to Stockport. The sun shone brightly, but the November breeze was nippy as she walked toward the shop. Maggie and Floyd arrived as she turned the key in the lock.

"I'm glad to see you looking more rested, Carey," Floyd commented, holding the door as the ladies stepped inside. "Today's the day, isn't it...for your crash course in tropical plants?"

"What are you talking about?" she asked, turning the thermostat up. Carey began filling the coffeepot with water.

"Maggie, didn't you tell me Carey was seeing Dr. Hensley this morning?" Floyd queried his wife with a teasing grin. Floyd was a tall, silver-haired man whose cheeks were ruddy, even when he *wasn't* teasing anyone.

"Oh, hush, old man. You're making a fuss over nothing. Carey's got enough on her mind without your making a to-do over some little meeting with a plant doctor. Probably just wants to pick her brain about ferns." Maggie gave Floyd a cross look as she dumped coins into the cash drawer.

"I'd forgotten all about Dr. Hensley. Thanks for reminding me." Carey leaned against Floyd, kissing him on the cheek. "You know, if you were my uncle, you'd be my favorite, Floyd."

The first hour and three quarters passed so quickly, Carey didn't even notice it was approaching ten o'clock.

"Better get a move on, if you're going to get to the college by ten, don't you think?" Maggie prodded, while fashioning three pink carnations into a corsage.

"Maggie, what would I do without you to keep me

15

on schedule? Sure you won't need me?" Carey pulled her jacket from its hook.

"Go on. Have fun." Maggie waved her hand toward the door.

Carey hugged her impulsively. "Thanks, Maggie. And you needn't look so innocent. I could tell you were just as interested in this *casual* meeting as Floyd was. I can just imagine what you must have said to him over the weekend."

"Oh, Carey. Dear child." Maggie kissed her on the cheek as if she were her own daughter. Her eyes glistened sadly, but her voice attempted a cheerful tone. "Now go on. You're only young once. I have a feeling Dr. Hensley has a lot more to offer than just plant talk."

Carey grabbed her hat and pulled her hair up under the knitted beret while checking her reflection in the mirror. Hurriedly, she touched a watermelon-pink gloss to her lips, then grabbed her bag and dashed out the door. As she half ran down the sidewalk to her rusty old Mustang, she wondered if Maggie and Floyd could be right. Did Alex Hensley have more on his mind than just plant talk?

Chapter Two

Carey parked near the science building and made her way toward the greenhouse. As she reached the door, she saw Alex, his back to her, engrossed in an inspection of several flowering plants. His broad shoulders filled out his tan corduroy, elbow-patched jacket. Before she could speak, Alex glanced toward the door, spotting her.

"There you are. Come on in." Alex's hazel eyes gleamed at her from beneath his thick brows. "What do you think of this Heliconia?" He held up an exotic looking plant bearing one colorful blossom.

"It's beautiful. Reminds me a little of Bird..."

"Of-Paradise?"

"Yes. That's it."

"Good. It's supposed to."

"Oh?"

Alex set the Heliconia down among several others like it. "Some Florida growers are experimenting with it. They think it may be a less expensive alternative to Bird-of-Paradise."

"I really don't pretend to know the first thing about exotic plants," Carey admitted without compunction.

"Good. Then I'll take plenty of time to teach you all

17

about them," Alex promised. His eyes met and held hers for a long moment, then he continued down the aisle between the benches. "This is a *Dionaea muscipula*, or Venus flytrap."

"Do they really eat flies?"

"Or hamburger. Watch." Alex took a small plastic bag from his jacket pocket and tossed a tiny ball of ground beef between two outward flaring leaves. They quickly snapped shut.

"Amazing. I suppose they import these from the tropical jungles of South America."

"Would you believe the bogs of the Carolinas? Then there's sensitive plant. Run your finger along the leaves." Alex grasped her hand. His large hand was warm and strong, wrapped around her chilled one. He moved her index finger along a feathered leaf. The edges curled together at her touch.

Carey realized that being with Alex was like being with an old, dear friend. Just knowing him made her feel comfortable, but Carey didn't understand why.

"I'd like to treat you to lunch," Alex mentioned, after he had shown her the bird's-nest fungus, fluffy ruffles, and staghorn ferns.

"I really should get back," Carey hedged, checking her watch. "You've already been generous with your time."

"My pleasure," he said meaningfully, "but since you'll have to eat anyway, why not with me?"

Carey thought about her own plans—drive straight home, whip together a cold meat sandwich, and sit at the table alone. "You just talked me into it," she brightened. "But nothing fancy. A hamburger would be fine. Can we meet at Burger Haven? That way I can go right back to work when we're done. I really do have a lot of work waiting for me."

"You drive a hard bargain, but," he winked once, and his smile showed even, white teeth, "it's a deal."

"Have some of my fries," Alex offered, as they sat at the tiny window table. "Carey, I'm going to be taking care of my brother Ben's two kids Saturday night. Thought I'd take them to a movie. They're surprisingly well-behaved for a four- and six-year-old. If you're not—"

"I'd love to," Carey blurted out, then bit her lip. They both chuckled. "I miss being around children so much since I left my teaching job," she hastily explained.

Wednesday morning arrived cold and a little snowy. After waiting on a customer who placed a wire service order, Carey looked up to see Gavin Jack backing through the side door. As he swung around, she saw that he carried a pail loaded with long-stemmed roses. Without a word, Gavin headed straight toward the cooler.

Quickly, Carey opened the register drawer and extracted an unmarked envelope from beneath the cash tray. "I believe this brings us up to date." Praying silently that her hand would stop shaking, she held the envelope out to Gavin as he returned to the door. "And thank you for the lovely fruit basket," she quickly added. "It was very thoughtful of you."

"You're welcome," he muttered. Gavin hesitated, then accepted the envelope from Carey, but his eyes never met hers. He tapped one end of the envelope on the counter, then extracted a knife from his pocket, and carefully slit open the other end.

Uneasily, she waited while he counted the contents of the envelope twice. Finally, he slid the bills back into the envelope and tossed it onto the counter.

"Considering your circumstances, I can carry you for

another week or two," he stated in a quiet tone. He moved toward the side door, but Carey swiftly scooped the payment from the counter and went after him.

"Oh, no you won't!" she exclaimed adamantly. "Last week you made it clear that our account was unacceptably behind. I don't need your sympathy, Mr. Jack; I need your roses. Here. Take it!" She followed him through the door into the cold air, grabbing him by the sleeve of his black leather jacket, and thrust the envelope toward him.

He removed her hand from his arm, squeezing it mercilessly. His black eyes bored hard into her. "Don't be foolhardy, Carey. When a break comes your way, take it." For a moment, his eyes searched hers, and the dark shards softened to warm liquid pools, making her wonder about his innermost thoughts. Finally, his steely grip relaxed, and he dropped her hand.

Carey shivered as she watched Gavin jump into his van and drive away.

"Everything all right, dear?" Maggie inquired.

"Fine. I guess," Carey answered as she tossed the envelope beneath the cash tray.

"Some tea to warm you?" Maggie poured hot water onto a tea bag in Carey's cup.

"Thanks." Carey blew across the surface, then sipped the steaming brew. "Maggie, what do you know about Jack Brothers Roses?"

"I know that Gavin runs the place now that his father and uncle are both gone." Maggie sipped at her coffee. "Floyd's sister over in Brighton used to know the family quite well. They went to the same church." She regarded Carey over the top of her cup. "He seems kind of rough around the edges, but my guess is, Gavin Jack's not half as tough as he looks, know what I mean?" Carey nodded.

She thought back to her childhood when her father had taken her with him to see the roses at Jack Brothers. It was located in Medeena, a small town about twelve miles from Stockport. She wondered if it had changed much over the years.

Maggie and Carey worked diligently on the floral pieces for the college banquet tables, but by closing time on Friday, it was evident that they would have to return after dinner to finish the orders in time for Saturday's delivery.

"Thanks for coming in extra, Maggie. Otherwise, I'd have been here all night trying to finish these in time."

"Oh, honey, you're welcome." She grinned. "Else I'd just be sitting around in front of the TV with Floyd."

"Oh, no. Poor Floyd. I didn't mean to swipe his companion." Carey frowned as she poked a long-stemmed rose into her arrangement.

"Now hush. He's in good company. He went to the bowling alleys to watch his pals bowl." Maggie quickly filled in the vacant spots of her centerpiece with fern, and added a little college pennant on a stick as the finishing touch.

Carey realized it would take a long time before she was as efficient at arranging flowers as Maggie. Her world from the age of ten on had always centered on music. Her beginning instrumental students could always count on her for encouragement, but now Carey was functioning in a different world. It would take her years to learn as much about the florist business as she already knew about music and teaching young students.

What plans could God have for her life, now that she was forced to function in a situation she knew so little about? With more than a little anxiety, she asked God to show her why her world had been so unfairly turned upside down.

"Thinking about that dashing Dr. Hensley, I suspect." Maggie's teasing accusation cut into the silence temporarily surrounding them. "You never did say, and it's none of my business, but I bet you'll be seeing more of him."

"Maggie, you're a frustrated matchmaker. You know that? But just to ease your mind, I'm helping him baby-sit tomorrow night."

A shocked and puzzled look flickered across Maggie's face. Carey threw her head back and laughed.

"No, they're not *his* kids. They're his *brother's*."

"Whew," Maggie chuckled, wiping imaginary perspiration from her brow. "You know, child," her expression grew serious, "you worry me. You should be out with others your age. Not cooped in here on a Friday night working your head off."

Carey shrugged. "You know what old Ben Franklin used to say: 'Take care of business, and your business will take care of *you*.' Responsibilities come first. These orders will give us a start on catching up with the bills."

Saturday was a very busy day, as Carey helped Floyd deliver the flowers for the college banquet. Before she even had a chance to think about it, she found herself preparing for her evening with Alex.

Carey chose a white sweater of lambs wool and angora, pairing it with her oxford gray wool split skirt. As she zipped her tall black leather boots, she heard Alex pull into the driveway.

"You look lovely tonight, Carey," Alex commented as he held her coat. "Mmm, your hair smells delicious," he murmured, holding it up as Carey's coat settled onto her shoulders.

Carey's eyes shone as she met Alex's appreciative

gaze. His mustache and beard were very carefully trimmed, and his clean masculine fragrance drifted pleasingly around her.

"I like your cologne," she mentioned, inhaling the scent. "It really suits you."

As Carey buttoned her coat, Alex leaned forward and planted a gentle kiss on her cheek.

Alex's kiss was so natural, it was as if Carey had been kissed by him a hundred times before. Being near Alex made her feel secure, and she liked that feeling.

"This is Scotty, and this little one is Jody." Alex introduced Carey as she settled on the front seat of the car beside him.

"Hi, Scotty and Jody."

"Hi, Carey. Gee, Uncle Alex. She sure is pretty. You gonna marry her?" Scotty innocently asked.

"Scotty, enough," Alex gently remonstrated, casting a sidelong glance at Carey. With any other man, Carey imagined she would have blushed deeply, but not with Alex. She smiled at Scotty.

"Jody, you're quiet tonight," Carey observed. Jody hid her face against her older brother's arm. "Aww. You're awfully pretty, in your pink jacket." Carey gently stroked the four-year-old's angel blond hair.

"We're going to see *Cinderella*. Have you ever seen *Cinderella*, Carey?" Scotty wanted to know.

"Oh yes. It's one of my favorite movies. Is this your first time to see it, Scotty?"

"No, but Jody's never seen it. You'll like it, Jody, I promise."

The seven o'clock showing was crowded with tots and their parents. Once Carey and the children were settled into their seats, Alex went to the lobby for popcorn and drinks. All too soon the movie was over, and

Carey helped zip and fasten the children into their outerwear for the trip to Alex's apartment.

Alex lived on the upper floor of a two-story older home on College Street. "In fact, I often leave the car in the driveway and walk to campus," he explained to Carey as they drove the few short blocks from the theater. "The science building isn't even a ten-minute walk from here."

"Uncle Alex, will you give me a ride like a horsey?" Scotty begged, when everyone had shed their coats.

"You're getting a little old for that, don't you think, Scotty?"

Jody, who had become quite comfortable with Carey, crawled up on her lap as they sat on the davenport.

"I think I know someone who's ready for a nap," Alex said, noticing Jody's yawn.

"Do I have to?" she whined. "Can you tell me a story first, Uncle Alex?"

A while later, after the children had settled on Alex's bed to nap until their parents came, Alex made coffee.

"You're a natural with them," Carey commented, sitting at the tiny table in Alex's kitchen.

He poured the coffee, then sat across from her. "They love you, too, Carey," he said almost reverently.

Carey only smiled. She had to admit that in the short time she'd known them, she adored Alex's niece and nephew.

The phone rang, and Alex quickly answered it. "Hello? Just a moment, please." Alex covered the mouthpiece with his hand. "It's for you. A woman."

"Hello?"

"Carey? I feel so awful calling you like this."

"Maggie? What is it? What's wrong? You sound out of breath."

"*I'm* fine, but something's gone wrong at the

greenhouse. The alarm rang, and Floyd's not here. He's visiting his sister in Brighton."

"Don't worry, Maggie. I'm on my way."

"What is it?" Alex asked, replacing the phone on the hook.

"I'm sorry. I have to check on the greenhouse. The alarm system has gone off."

"Shouldn't you call the police to go with you?" Alex hurriedly suggested.

"It's not a burglar alarm, it's a temperature alarm. The greenhouse has gotten too cold. The furnace probably went off." Carey quickly slipped on her coat.

Years ago, Carey's father had installed a temperature sensitive alarm in the greenhouse that rang at home and at the Emery's when the temperature dropped below a certain point.

"Here. Take my car." Alex held out the keys.

She hesitated. "Sure you don't mind?"

"No, of course not. I wish I could come with you, but—" he nodded toward the bedroom where the children were napping.

"I know. I'm so sorry." Carey opened the door, then faced him once again before leaving. "I've had a lovely time, Alex. Thank you."

As she drove across town, Carey wondered if she'd be able to get an emergency repair service to fix the furnace before permanent damage was done. The whole poinsettia crop was at stake. Lose that, and the business would surely go under. She prayed for help as she drove.

Within ten minutes, Carey was inside the greenhouse, looking at the thermometer. Already, the temperature was below forty-five degrees. She wondered how long it would take for it to drop another thirteen degrees.

She grabbed the phone book and turned to the yellow pages. Carey left a message with the closest repair service making weekend emergency repairs, then put on the tea kettle. It would be a long, cold night.

Carey sipped her hot chocolate. The passing minutes seemed like an eternity. She paced the floor, then compulsively tidied up the countertop and desk. Finally, she phoned the repair service again. They assured her that someone would be there within the hour. She was afraid to check the thermometer again.

Carey moved the desk chair so she could rest her head against the wall. Horrid, depressing thoughts drifted through her subconscious as she dozed off.

With the sudden, loud banging on the side door, she bolted from the chair, thinking the repairman had arrived.

"Carey, are you all right?" the loud voice demanded as she approached the door. "Carey! Open up!"

"Gavin Jack! What are you doing here?"

"Let me in before I rip this door off the hinges!"

His dark, leathery figure behind the glass was almost frightening, but she did as he demanded.

"You O.K.?" he asked again.

"Yes, fine. Why?"

"The way you were sitting there, I thought...never mind. Your furnace. Where is it?"

"It's back by the—"

"Show me."

Swiftly, Carey led Gavin down the long aisle of the first greenhouse, through a storage room, into the potting room behind, then pointed to the few steps leading down to the furnace.

Gavin grabbed a flashlight from a shelf and was on his knees, inspecting the rear of the furnace. Within moments, Carey heard the furnace click on. Silently, she said a prayer of thanks for Gavin's unexpected intervention. Gavin continued checking the furnace with the flashlight for a few minutes, then confronted her.

"When was the last time the filters were changed?"

"I...don't know," she answered hesitantly.

"You'd better learn the basics of furnace maintenance if you expect to stay in business," he said, shaking his head.

"What was wrong?"

"The pilot light went out."

Carey saw lights in the driveway and moved to the window in the storage room door. Gavin followed.

"It's the repairman. He'll replace the filters for me."

"That furnace needs a good cleaning, too," Gavin informed her.

Carey showed the repairman to the furnace room. Gavin followed him down the steps. The furnace room barely accommodated one repairman, let alone an onlooker. Carey was perturbed by Gavin's overbearance. He told the man to replace the filters, clean the furnace, and inspect its overall condition.

While they were talking, Carey checked on the poinsettia crop. The plants seemed to be holding up without any damage. The temperature hovered around forty degrees, and she praised God for bringing the heat on in time to keep the greenhouses above freezing. She returned to the potting room.

Several minutes later, Gavin left the furnace room and stood beside her.

"How did you get involved in this?" Carey asked, trying her best to sound self-confident.

"I saw the office lights on as I drove by and got suspicious. Your father had problems with break-ins, so I decided to check around." Gavin regarded her with dark, intense eyes. "You almost lost your business tonight, young lady," he admonished.

Carey's chin dropped. *O Lord*, she silently prayed, *I need your support every moment if I'm going to succeed.*

"What are you going to do about it?"

"Pardon?"

"I said, what are you going to do about it? Really, you shouldn't be so frivolous about managing this business."

"Frivolous!" Carey was instantly infuriated by Gavin's words. "How can you possibly accuse me of that when you..." she faltered.

Gavin stood silent. An amused, upward curl touched one corner of his mouth. He seemed to know something she did not know, but Carey barely caught this subtlety, her anger so consumed her.

A disturbance near the front of the shop interrupted the confrontation. Carey ran through the aisle of the front greenhouse. Gavin took the opposite aisle arriving just ahead of her at the door separating the greenhouse from the shop. He was through it and in the office first.

"I tell you, I'm a friend of Ms. McIlwain," the man insisted.

"Alex! What's going on?"

"Carey, will you please tell this officer I'm not some Saturday night burglar?" The policeman wrenched Alex's arms behind his back.

Carey glanced at Gavin long enough to catch the steel hard look on his face. Muscles, coiled like a tightly wound spring, tensed beneath his leather exterior.

"I stopped by to check your doors and found this man trying to enter," the policeman explained.

"It's all right, Don. He's a friend of mine. Everything's under control."

Reluctantly, he released Alex. A long-time village policeman and friend of Carey's father, Don eyed Gavin suspiciously.

"Gavin stopped by to help. He supplies my roses," Carey explained.

"I'll get back to my rounds, then. Just call if you have any trouble, Carey."

"Thank you, Don."

As Carey opened her mouth to introduce Alex to Gavin, the phone rang. She grabbed the extension next to the arranging table.

"McIlwain Greenhouses."

"Carey, is everything O.K.?"

"Yes, Floyd, everything's fine. Thank you."

"Did the temperature get too low?"

"No, the furnace is going fine."

"Good. Just give a holler if you need me."

"Will do, Floyd. See you Monday."

Carey observed the two men during her brief phone conversation. Neither spoke a word. She wanted to shake Gavin by the shoulders for the intimidating scowl he had given Alex. Alex had shifted his weight uncomfortably, watching Carey as she spoke to Floyd, but avoiding eye contact with Gavin.

"Gavin, this is *Doctor* Alex Hensley from the college science department," she explained, hoping the emphasis on "Doctor" would give Alex credibility in Gavin's eyes. "Alex, Gavin Jack, owner of Jack Brothers Roses."

"Pleasure, Gavin," Alex's hand shot out. Slowly, Gavin unfolded his arms and accepted the handshake.

"Alex, how did you get here?"

"I had my brother drop me off when he came for the kids. I wanted to check and make sure everything was all right." Alex glanced uneasily at Gavin.

"Gavin got the heat on. The repairman is cleaning and checking the furnace." Carey reached into her

29

pocket for Alex's car keys. "Thanks for the use of your car. I don't know what I'd have done without it."

The repairman entered the office. "I don't think you'll have any more problems this winter, but if you do, just give me a call." He handed her an itemized bill. Carey's eyes widened when she saw the bottom line. She shot a quick glance at Gavin before she could remind herself that he had probably saved her business tonight.

Gavin took the bill out of her hand. He waited until the repairman was gone, then commented, "Small price to pay for a poinsettia crop." He tossed the bill on the counter.

"Let me walk you home, if you're done here, Carey," Alex offered. His smooth tone quelled her anger with Gavin.

"Thank you. I'd like that." She retrieved her coat from the desk chair, giving Gavin a look of dismissal as she passed in front of him and handed it to Alex.

"I'll see you Wednesday, as usual, Carey," Gavin said, his tone implying she had a date with him rather than a standing rose order. Alex's eyebrow arched at the remark.

"I have the strongest urge to wring his neck," Carey said to Alex, as they walked to the house.

"Looks like you have to wait until Wednesday," Alex dryly observed.

"I know I should be grateful to him, but his attitude really irritates me." They mounted the porch steps, and Carey turned to Alex.

Alex's soft, hazel eyes looked even more mellow in the dimness of the pale, November moonlight. As he drew Carey closer, she caught the scent of his cologne, the kind she would never grow tired of. But as his lips drew near to give her a caressing good-night kiss, it was the image of Gavin Jack that invaded her private thoughts.

Gavin Jack! How Carey wished he would simply drop his unexplainable interest in her business. Yet, Gavin possessed a strange magnetism, which attracted and repelled her at the same time.

Alex held her as if she were a fragile china doll, then slowly released her.

"Would you like to—" Carey began, but was interrupted.

"Thank you for coming with us to the movie tonight, Carey. Jody and Scotty had a *wonderful* time because of you."

"You're welcome. I, uh, enjoyed it as much as they did, I'm sure."

"Good night, Carey."

"Good night." Carey's eyes followed Alex as he moved briskly toward his car. She wondered why he had left so abruptly. Surely he knew she was about to invite him inside when he interrupted her.

She felt her pockets for her house key.

The weeks went by. Carey saw Alex occasionally. Sometimes she helped him babysit the children; other times they attended a play or a concert at the college fine arts center.

Gavin Jack appeared once a week on Wednesday mornings to deliver the rose order. Each week, Carey handed him an envelope with payment in full, and each week, Gavin counted the contents twice, returned the bills to the envelope, and placed it on the counter.

During the month of December, Carey kept the shop open after dinner, which meant she and Maggie spent many late evenings preparing arrangements for the Christmas rush. Carey's cousin, Gail, had agreed to work part-time during the holiday season, but even with added help, the overtime began to wear Carey down.

One morning, she awoke with an extremely sore throat and a bad cold developed in her chest. Four days later Carey arose with a shaking chill. She also noticed sharp chest pains and a bad cough, which had not bothered her previously. She told herself she was just chillier than usual because of the extremely cold, windy weather. She made herself some hot chocolate and dressed for work.

"Carey, I *wish* you'd take some time off," Maggie pleaded after hearing Carey's bad cough.

"That's the fifth or sixth time you've said that," Carey gently pointed out, knowing Maggie was right. But the responsibility of running the business through the busiest season of the year prevented Carey from considering taking any time off for illness.

"I know I'm repeating myself, dear, but you don't seem to pay any attention to me. Gail and I can handle the shop for a couple of days. You need your rest."

"In another ten days the rush will be over, then I'll rest." Carey coughed hard into a tissue, then noticed she had coughed up blood. She discreetly turned her back to Maggie so she would not see the concern on her own face.

"At least see a doctor, child. You can do that much for yourself."

"If it will make you happy, I'll call Dr. Thompson."

"No need to call him. Just go to his office at three o'clock," Maggie urged, as Carey reached for the phone book.

"He won't see me without an appointment," Carey mumbled, flipping through the pages.

"I know. I've already made one. You're scheduled at

3 p.m. Now will you please go home and rest until then? I don't want to catch what you've got." Maggie ushered her by the shoulders to the coat rack.

"I'll call Gail." Carey turned toward the phone, but Maggie stopped her.

"I've already done that. She'll be here any minute. Now go!" Like a concerned grandmother, Maggie helped Carey into her coat and wrapped her scarf securely around her sore throat.

Gail came in the door of the shop as Carey was leaving. "You look awful, Cousin. Go straight to bed and don't worry about a thing. Maggie and I can handle it."

At home, Carey stuck a thermometer in her mouth, then snuggled down under her electric blanket. She had to admit to herself she had never felt this rotten with a cold. The thermometer registered 102. She laid her head on her pillow and set her alarm clock for two-thirty.

Carey's next recollection was of the phone ringing. At first, she thought it was the alarm clock, so she picked it up to shut it off, then noticed it said only twelve-twenty. She had been asleep for over two hours, but felt as if she could barely get up to answer the phone, which kept on ringing. She pulled on her robe and stepped into the kitchen.

"Carey? You all right? It's Alex."

"I was asleep, Alex. Sorry it took me so long to answer."

"I'm sorry I woke you, but when Maggie said you were really ill, I thought I'd call and ask if there's anything I can do. Have you eaten anything today?"

"No."

"You can't get well if you don't eat. Leave your door unlocked. I'll be over in a few minutes."

"Thanks, Alex, but I can manage. Alex?"

Chapter Three

The line was already dead. Carey didn't want to see anyone today, let alone Alex. She dialed his number, but he didn't answer.

Carey unlocked her door, then went to the bathroom to comb her hair and brush her teeth. Even her favorite cinnamon-with-mouthwash toothpaste tasted horrid. She pulled the collar of her plush aqua robe up around her neck, then settled under an afghan on the couch.

Only a few minutes later, she heard the sounds of Alex's arrival.

"When did your cold get worse?" Alex interrogated her as he worked the lid off of a large styrofoam cup of soup.

"This morning, I guess," Carey answered weakly.

"I knew when we were out Friday you felt worse than you were willing to admit. I never should have let you go anywhere."

"Alex, stop blaming yourself."

"Here, try this," he said, placing a lap tray in front of her containing chicken noodle soup and saltines.

Alex still wore his steel-blue insulated jacket. It made his well-developed torso seem even larger, and in her misery, Carey felt comforted with Alex's hulking frame nearby.

"I'll be back for you at quarter-to-three."

"Who told you about—"

"Finish that, then back to bed. I'll see you later."

Carey was too tired to argue. Besides, Alex was gone before she could say anything more.

At two-thirty, Carey pulled on some old jeans and a lambs wool sweater. When she checked the mirror, she was horrified at the red lines in her eyes. Halfheartedly, she applied some blusher and lip gloss, then answered Alex's knock on the door.

Alex placed his arm securely around Carey's waist as he helped her into his car. For once, Carey was glad to let someone drive for her. Her self-sufficiency and independent spirit seemed to evaporate with the onset of her illness.

"Carey McIlwain? This way please." Carey followed the nurse to an examining room in the outpatient clinic. Located in a wing off the hospital, the clinic was only a block from her home on West Avenue.

The nurse took Carey's temperature, blood pressure, and pulse. "Dr. Thompson will be with you in a moment. Please undress to the waist, and put this on." The nurse handed her a short paper cover-up.

Carey sat on the table waiting for Dr. Thompson. She began to shiver again because the paper cover-up was so flimsy.

"Well, Carey, it's been a few years since you've been in here, hasn't it?" Dr. Thompson asked, as he closed the door.

"Haven't been back since you took out my tonsils. You must've done a good job, huh?" Carey tried to joke, but her spirit sagged.

"So you've had a bad cold for a few days, and now

you've got a fever," the white-haired doctor commented.

"That Maggie." Carey shook her head.

"Let's see." Dr. Thompson said, pulling the paper cover-up up enough to apply the cold stethoscope on her chest. "Take a deep breath. Again." He switched to her back. "Inhale. Again. Hmm."

Carey coughed, wincing at the pain in her chest. Again, she coughed up blood.

"Carey, you've got to go straight to bed and stay there," Dr. Thompson ordered.

"But I have a business to run," Carey countered.

"You won't be around to run it if you don't take care of yourself. You have bronchopneumonia. Drop your jeans. I'm going to give you a shot."

"How long before I can go back to work?"

"Sometime after Christmas. Maybe by the first of the year."

"But Dr...." Carey protested.

"No buts. This is a small town, Carey, and I'd better not hear about you going over to that greenhouse and working until I say it's O.K. Got that, young lady? Now, do as I say."

When Carey came out, Alex conferred with the doctor. "What do you think?"

"Make this young woman rest, will you? She's got pneumonia."

"I thought so." Alex shook his head.

"It's contagious, so keep your distance." Dr. Thompson addressed Carey. "I want nothing but bed rest for you for the next two weeks. Here's a prescription, and Doris will set up another appointment following Christmas."

Carey silently slumped onto the passenger's seat of Alex's car. Pneumonia couldn't have hit her at a worse time. Aside from the rush at the shop, she hadn't even started her own personal Christmas preparations. And Dr. Thompson expected her to just lie around the house? There *had* to be another way to get over this disease. Though her thoughts flew quickly from one possibility to another, her body told her Dr. Thompson was right. She had to stay in bed.

"I'll take the prescription to the pharmacy for you," Alex said, as he pulled into Carey's driveway. His words pierced her thoughts.

Carey touched her hand to his. "Thank you, Alex." She wanted to say more. She wanted to tell him how much she appreciated his thoughtful help, his concern for her, his companionship over the past few weeks. But a hard lump formed in her throat, and she didn't trust her voice.

Alex saw her to the door, then left immediately for the medicine. Carey slowly undressed and plumped her pillows on one end of the couch. As she lay beneath the afghan daydreaming, a thought suddenly struck her. This was Monday afternoon—why wasn't Alex teaching his classes? He was so devoted to his profession, apparently having no other interests aside from spending time with Scotty and Jody when the opportunity presented itself.

Tears stung Carey's eyes. She was touched by Alex's concern for her. She wondered, too, whether the pneumonia, which had debilitated her, had made her so depressed. She would not have acquired these responsibilities if her parents were still alive to share this Christmas with her. She grabbed a tissue and dabbed at her eyes. *Alex is such a good friend*, she thought, as she heard him return from the pharmacy.

"I'll be by tomorrow with your lunch. Can you manage breakfast on your own?" Alex asked, after watching her swallow an antibiotic as if she were a small child who needed mothering.

"Of course. I'm not *that* sick." She brightened, hoping Alex would believe she was still independent in spite of the pneumonia. "Alex," she spoke his name pensively, "what about your Monday afternoon classes?"

"That's one of the benefits of having an assistant," Alex grinned. He studied her silently for a moment, then asked, "Have you spoken with your brother lately?"

"No. I never seem to catch Todd in, and he hasn't called for some time. I suppose he's busy preparing for finals. It's the end of their term, I think."

"Maybe he could help out at the greenhouse over the weekend, or at least as soon as his exams are finished. Why don't you call him? The business is *his* responsibility, too, Carey."

"Maybe I should. I really don't expect much help from that quarter though, Alex."

"Perhaps that's the problem." Alex's brows arched poignantly.

Carey rested on the couch throughout the afternoon, occasionally drifting into a light sleep. Much to her dismay, each time she dozed off, she envisioned herself having an argument with Todd!

"This is ridiculous," she told herself, leaning up on one elbow. Carey shuffled into the kitchen and thumbed through her mother's personal phone directory until she located Todd's number, then dialed.

"Todd? This is Carey."

"Hi, Sis. Hey, I'm glad you called. I was just thinking about calling you."

"You were?"

"Yeah. You wouldn't have any extra cash, would you?"

"Todd, I wish I did…"

"It's just till the end of the term. I'm getting a new student loan next semester, then I'll pay you right back."

Carey asked, "How much did you have in mind?"

"Carey, your voice sounds funny. I guess it's just the connection. Could you loan me a couple hundred?"

"A couple *hundred*?"

"You'll get it back, I promise. I know you don't think so after all those other times I borrowed from you, but this is different."

"Todd, can you get home this weekend to help at the greenhouse?"

"Gee, Carey. I'd help if I could, but I've got exams to study for. You know how it is. Now, how about it. Can I count on you for the cash?"

"Can I count on you for some *help*?" Carey heard no response. She didn't believe Todd would study. He never had in the past, but always scraped by somehow. "Todd, I'm sick and can't work for a while. The Emerys need help, especially Floyd with all the deliveries. Can't you reconsider?"

"Like I said, Carey, I'm tied up. I promised Amy we'd go ski—"

"*Skiing*?" Carey was incensed. "If there's no business for you to take over after graduation, Todd, you'll at least have fantastic memories of a weekend on the slopes. Good-bye." She dropped the phone onto the cradle.

Carey regretted her brusk manner with Todd only for a moment. Although he was all the family she had, she realized Alex was right. Todd should be expected to pitch in.

Perhaps Todd had always gotten off too easily. As a small boy, his impish looks had charmed adults into letting him get, and get away with, anything he wanted. Now that Todd was an adult it seemed things were no different.

The period of Carey's confinement passed. During the first two days, she was so weary and sick, she didn't mind Dr. Thompson's restrictions.

Carey's aunt prepared and sent dinners over to her, and Alex stopped by on Tuesday with her lunch. Even friends from church, who had come to the flower shop looking for her, stopped by to offer help and chat for a few minutes, easing her loneliness and depression a little.

By Wednesday morning, Carey felt more rested. Her spirits lifted. She reached for her Bible, believing she could again, in good faith, open her communication with God. During the busy days and evenings at the greenhouse since her parents' death, then in the early part of her illness, Carey's daily devotions had halted.

When she turned to Psalms, many passages offered her comfort. As she read, her anger with God for taking her parents, then allowing her to become ill, slowly evaporated. She praised Him for being with her even when she had not acknowledged Him. For the first time in weeks, a peace came over Carey, completely encompassing her, healing her wounded heart.

The peacefulness of her meditations were suddenly shattered by an urgent pounding on her door!

Panic gripped her as she heard the doorknob turn, for she had left the door unlocked this morning so Alex could enter easily with her lunch. She sat motionless on the couch.

"Gavin! What are you doing here?"

"Got any vases?" He held at least a dozen and a half red roses, blossoms down, as he glanced about the living room and dining area.

"In the kitchen." Carey started to get up.

"You stay put, young lady," he ordered, pointing with his fistful of roses. "Where in the kitchen?"

"Above the refrigerator."

Carey listened as Gavin drew water in a vase. Her heart still pounded, but she knew it was no longer because he had startled her, but because he was *here*. Her eyes returned to her opened Bible, but her thoughts were elsewhere.

Gavin entered the living room carrying a vase of artistically arranged long-stemmed red roses. He cleared a spot on the TV and set the vase there, then took a seat on the edge of her father's recliner.

"Next time I see you, I want to see two of those roses back in your cheeks. What's the matter with you, anyway? Don't you know when to ease up?" Gavin leaned toward her, leather cap in hand, his dark penetrating eyes trained on her.

Carey blushed deeply beneath his gaze. Though her long, plush robe covered her fully, she felt embarrassingly undressed.

"The roses are lovely. Thank you," Carey said, looking for an excuse to avoid his gaze. She took a deep breath and summoned her spunk. "Did Maggie give you the envelope? I told her to pay you," she stated.

"She gave it to me," he said, pausing, "and I gave it back."

"As usual. Why don't you just accept it and stop making me feel like I'm always in your debt?"

"Look, I'm just trying to help you stay afloat. We'll see how McIlwain Greenhouses gets through the holidays, then we'll settle up."

Carey studied Gavin for a moment, wondering about the man behind the rough exterior. Was there a secret soft spot somewhere? Perhaps he had an area of tenderness he tried to keep hidden from the rest of the world, but which occassionally surfaced in spite of his gruffness.

"Carey, tell me something. How are you going to survive?" She couldn't mistake the doubt in his question. "You're a teacher, aren't you?"

"*Was.* I may have a lot to learn about the florist business, but I have faith. We'll get by. The Lord will see to it."

"Just like He saw to your parents' accident and your pneumonia?"

"What a horrible thing to say! If you knew the first thing about Him, you'd know that the Lord *never* turns His back on those who love Him." In an instant Carey knew she had spoken too hotly. "I'm sorry. Please forgive me."

Gavin rose to leave.

"What's to forgive? You have your faith, I have mine." Gavin pulled on his cap and was gone without another word.

Oh, Carey, you blew it! Carey chastised herself. *If only you'd thought before you spoke. You had the perfect opportunity to share your faith. Instead, you scared him off.*

Carey sat there, her Bible still open to Psalms, wondering. *Just what is your faith, Gavin Jack?*

Little by little, Carey's energy returned. Each day, she felt stronger. She began to decorate the house for Christmas, doing only a small amount at a time, taking long rest breaks.

Whenever she looked at the vase of red roses, she

wondered if Gavin knew they symbolized God's everlasting love. The blossoms were wide open now, and the petals had started dropping, but their fragrance lingered. She prayed every day that Gavin would some day come to know the one true loving God.

As Carey's Christmas spirit rose, she compiled a list of gifts. There were so many people to remember this year—those who had pitched in for her at the greenhouse, and of course Alex and his niece and nephew.

Carey dared not think of doing any shopping herself after Dr. Thompson's stern warning, so she asked a member of her church to shop for her. Many of her church family had offered to help, and now she knew exactly what help she needed. Christmas was only a few days away, and Alex had already promised to be her Santa Claus and deliver the presents in return for her offer to wrap his gifts.

Two days before Christmas, Carey and Alex stood by her dining table. Beautiful foil-wrapped packages were piled in front of them.

"Looks like Santa's workshop," Alex teased, turning a bow-topped gift over in his hands.

"These all go to the greenhouse," she explained, pointing out one stack, "and those go to my aunt and uncle. Yours are—" The phone rang, interrupting her.

"Todd. When are you coming in? You're spending Christmas at Amy's?...Oh. Well, see you New Year's then. Merry Christmas, Todd. And tell Amy I wish her a merry one, too. Bye."

Carey tried to hide her hurt and disappointment over Todd's call as she returned to the gifts and Alex. "These are yours to your brother's family," she continued, much less enthusiastically than before.

"Carey, spend Christmas with me and my family,"

Alex urged, his soft hazel eyes searching hers.

His soothing voice smoothed her troubled emotions as his hand reached for hers. Gently, he held her small delicate hand between his, and Carey had to fight hard to keep back a tear. She cleared her throat, trying to rid it of the lump that had formed there.

"Alex, you're the sweetest man I know, but I don't want to impose on your family."

"You won't be imposing, Carey. In fact, my mother would be delighted to meet you. She's been after me for weeks to bring you with me some Sunday."

Alex's mother lived in Rochester. Every Sunday Alex took his mother to church, then stayed for dinner. Though he had asked Carey numerous times to join them, she had declined.

Now that she knew Todd would not be spending Christmas with her, Carey's outlook had dimmed. She simply could not face Christmas alone.

"Alex, I'd love to come, if you don't think it's too much of an intrusion."

Alex raised her hand to his lips and kissed it softly. The depth of emotion she saw in his eyes almost scared her.

"Careful," she half-whispered, as his lips moved from her hand to her cheek. "You'll catch my pneumonia."

"I don't care," he said huskily. "This is going to be the best Christmas in years."

Chapter Four

"Uncle Alex!"

"Carey!"

Scotty, then Jody, ran to meet Carey and Alex at the door.

"How's my big man today?" Alex asked, scooping Scotty off the floor.

"Carey, will you play house with me?" Jody tugged at Carey's hand.

"Not so fast, sweetheart," Carey chuckled, unwinding her neck scarf.

"Jody wants to play with her dumb doll," Scotty lamented. "Come on, Uncle Alex. Let's play truck driver."

"Hold on just a minute, Scotty." Alex helped Carey out of her coat.

"Hello, Carey. I'm Jenine, mother of the two whirlwinds." Petite, dark-haired Jenine hugged Carey's shoulders as if they were fast friends.

"You're one very fortunate woman."

"Some days, I'd trade those two for ten minutes of peace and quiet. They're really flying high today, but…"

"You wouldn't have it any other way." Carey finished.

"You're right," Jenine admitted, dark eyes twinkling

as she watched her youngsters dash across the room to their toys.

"Let's find Mother, shall we?" Alex suggested, guiding Carey toward the kitchen. Mrs. Hensley met them halfway.

"Mother, this is Carey McIlwain. Carey, my mother, Serita Hensley."

"Pleased to meet you." Mrs. Hensley smiled, taking in Carey's appearance with the eye of a practiced appraiser. "Sorry I didn't greet you at the door. My gravy was at a critical stage."

"I understand. I have yet to make gravy without lumps," Carey empathized, while mentally squirming under the older woman's scrutiny.

"Now, if you'll excuse me, the potatoes must be about to boil over." Mrs. Hensley returned to the kitchen before Carey could offer her assistance.

"So big brother finally got up the courage to bring you home. Hello, Carey. I'm Ben." Ben, a taller but less rugged version of his older brother, had entered from the den. "Think you can handle the Hensley clan for a day?"

"I'm sure of it." Carey said with a laugh.

Mrs. Hensley carried a silver gravy boat to the table, followed by Jenine carrying a basket piled high with dinner rolls.

"Can I help you?" Carey offered, thankful for Alex's reassuring squeeze of her hand.

"Perhaps you could carry in the vegetables, dear. Then if I can enlist Alex to carve the turkey, we're all set," Mrs. Hensley directed.

Jenine ushered the children to the bathroom to wash up. A semblance of holiday ritual settled in as everyone gathered at the table for the sumptuous meal.

The dinner table was impeccably set with sterling silver and bone china dishes, befitting the image Mrs. Hensley projected with her perfectly coiffed silver hair and designer-label, dusky-rose knit suit. In fact, the Hensley home reminded Carey of a page from *House Beautiful* with its elegant crystal chandelier suspended above the dining table and immaculate linens spread beneath the place settings.

Alex offered a blessing, then took carving knife in hand to lay precise slices of white meat on the platter. Mrs. Hensley placed turkey, dressing, and vegetables on each plate, then passed the side dishes.

Carey stifled a gasp as Jody unsteadily handed the cranberry sauce to her older brother, who came dangerously close to losing his grip before Jenine rescued it from him.

Following the delicious feast, Carey assisted Mrs. Hensley and Jenine with the cleanup, while Alex and Ben brought the gifts in from Alex's car. As Carey stood at the buffet in the dining room replacing utensils in Mrs. Hensley's silver chest, Jenine approached her in a rare moment of privacy.

"It's been years since Alex has brought a girlfriend home to meet Mother," Jenine spoke in low tones, glancing furtively into the kitchen where Mrs. Hensley stored serving dishes.

Carey looked questioningly into Jenine's impish, sparkling brown eyes. As Mrs. Hensley joined them, Jenine mouthed the word, "later" and turned to her mother-in-law.

"Thank you, dears, for your help. Perhaps the boys are ready in the living room with the gifts now. Shall we join them?"

As Carey entered the living room, she admired Mrs. Hensley's flair for interior decorating. Velvet moss-green draperies crisscrossed the picture window, enhancing the natural green of the perfectly shaped Christmas tree. Silvery white plush carpeting cushioned Carey's feet as she moved to the brocade sofa and found a place next to Alex.

Mounds of gifts surrounded Mrs. Hensley's Christmas tree, which projected a designer's care in the choice and placement of its ornaments. Coral velvet balls were evenly spaced among the branches. Strings of pink lights shimmered beneath a layer of carefully applied angel's hair. There was little in the picture perfect room to remind Carey of Christmases at her parents' home, or the quaint, handsewn felt Santas she and her brother hung on the tree year after year.

"Start with the children, dear." Mrs. Hensley directed her attention toward Ben, the self-appointed Santa.

"Good idea. A little something to occupy the rascals," he commented.

Scotty ripped eagerly into his package, revealing a toy gas station complete with pumps, cars, and service station attendants. He immediately set about arranging the pieces to suit himself.

Ben placed a huge carton at the feet of his diminutive daughter. Everyone smiled at the disbelief in the four-year-old's eyes when, a few moments later, Jody pulled out a Victorian dollhouse, complete with furnishings.

"Thanks, Uncle Alex. It's the bestest gift ever," she sang, running to his arms.

"Thank Carey, too. She gave you the furniture."

"Thank you, Carey," Jody said, hugging her excitedly.

Ben retrieved more packages from beneath the tree.

" 'To Carey. Fondest wishes for a very Merry Christmas. Alex.' " Ben read aloud.

A gleam of curiosity shone in Carey's eyes as she turned over the foil-wrapped parcel and eased off the red velvet ribbon. Aware that Alex observed her intensely, she opened the box and held up its contents.

"Thank you, Alex. How perfectly lovely. I hope to wear them in good health." She smiled as she examined the cornflower-blue mohair scarf, mittens, and stocking cap. They were exactly the kind of appropriate gift she expected from Alex.

"And for you, Alex, from your lovely lady friend." Ben handed Carey's gift to Alex.

Now it was Carey's turn to watch Alex's reaction. "Where did you ever find this?" he asked, astonishment coloring his tone as he opened the cover of a rare text on exotic plants.

"Thompson's located it for me. They have a book search service. They found it stashed in a corner of the publisher's warehouse."

"But I've tried for years to locate a copy of *Remington's Guide to Rare Species,* and the publisher always said it was out of print."

"Women have their ways, dear brother," Ben interjected knowingly. "Anyone for some brandy? Carey?"

"No thank you, Ben. I'd like some ginger ale, if you have it."

"Ginger ale?" he mocked sarcastically. "You've already picked up Alex's bad habit, I see."

"Scotty, Jody, wouldn't you like to give Carey her gifts?" Jenine smoothly changed the course of conversation while Ben filled old-fashioned glasses with ice and ginger ale.

Carey watched as the opened gifts piled beside her—a cloisonné necklace from Jody, matching earrings from Scotty, vellum stationery from Jenine and Ben, and an elegant gold pen and pencil set from Mrs. Hensley.

"From Carey, Mother," Alex explained, handing her the only package Carey had topped with a living red rose, insulating it against the cold in a triple layer of

49

foam. The packaging scheme had worked. The rose had not frozen en route to Mrs. Hensley. Carey intertwined her fingers nervously as Mrs. Hensley set the rose aside without comment and opened her last gift.

"How perfectly lovely," Mrs. Hensley observed, holding up the hand-crocheted, lace dresser scarf. "Did you stitch it yourself?"

"A relative made it for me," Carey answered, unable to read Mrs. Hensley's expression. Carey had wrapped the heirloom dresser scarf, her mother's handiwork, for Mrs. Hensley when she realized at the last minute she'd be spending Christmas day in her home. It was the only appropriate and affordable gift she could find on short notice, though it had cost her emotionally to give the piece away. With a sinking feeling, Carey watched Mrs. Hensley quickly return it to its box and place it to one side. Carey wondered if she'd paid too big a price for it, nonetheless.

"Daddy, will you take me sledding over at the park?" Scotty's question broke the awkward silence.

Ben glanced at Alex, then a mischievous look came into his eyes. "Tell you what, Scotty, if you can convince your Uncle Alex to go, then we'll show you what it was like to sled when we were your age."

"Please, Uncle Alex. Will you go?"

"Is that toboggan still in the rafters of the garage, Mother?" Alex's mouth twitched in amusement, making Carey wonder what antics the brothers silently planned.

Mrs. Hensley nodded.

"Carey, do you mind?" Alex asked. "We won't be gone too long. Just until Scotty gets cold."

"Play dollhouse with me, Carey," Jody begged.

"Of course, I'd love to," Carey insisted, joining Jody on the floor.

"I'll take you tobogganing after you're fully recovered from pneumonia," Alex promised, his dark brows arching mischievously.

"It's an experience you won't forget, I can assure you," Ben teased.

"I can hardly wait," Carey returned dryly.

Alex bent down and clasped her shoulder tenderly before the three males bundled themselves into overcoats and snowpants and headed for a nearby sledding hill.

With the men away, conversation in the living room turned naturally toward topics of interest to women. Mrs. Hensley and Jenine did most of the talking, while Carey limited her participation to comments interspersed with those of Jody's make-believe dollhouse people.

"I think I'm ready for a cup of coffee," Mrs. Hensley announced. "Carey? Jenine?"

"No, thank you, Mrs. Hensley."

"I'll join you, Mother," Jenine offered, disappearing with Mrs. Hensley into the kitchen.

Carey leaned back against the couch as she watched Jody rearrange, piece by piece, every room in her dollhouse. She could hear Jenine and Alex's mother chatting more like old bridge partners than mother-in-law and daughter-in-law, but their conversation soon receded to the back of Carey's mind.

She assessed Alex's qualities—his never-failing thoughtfulness, the time and concern he'd shown during her illness, his insistence that she share this special holiday with his family, his unquestionably distinguished appearance, and his taut, slightly stocky build.

But seeing the Hensley home, the showpiece decorating schemes, and experiencing the close scrutiny of Alex's mother made Carey wonder if perhaps she had less in common with Alex than she had originally thought. They shared a similar faith, it was true, but so much more contributed to an enduring, loving relationship.

Absently, she reached for the box containing her mother's dresser scarf, now Mrs. Hensley's, and fingered the finely crocheted cotton stitches. Perhaps the differences between her family and Alex's were greater than she had imagined.

"Know something?" Jody half whispered, breaking into Carey's reverie as she rearranged the Victorian sofa in the parlor of her dollhouse. "You're more fun than Grandma, Carey."

"How's that, sweetheart?"

"You play house with me. Stuff like that. Grandma never has time to play with us."

"What do you and Scotty do when you visit your grandma, Jody?"

Jody shrugged and sighed with a grimace. "She teaches us proper manners. She says it's important."

"And your grandmother is right."

"But playing make-believe is more fun," Jody whined.

"Oh, but you can learn a lot from your grandmother about good manners, and it's something that will last a lifetime." As she finished the sentence, Carey noticed Mrs. Hensley had slipped into the living room, and she wondered how much of the conversation she had overheard. Carey sensed that Mrs. Hensley was keenly observing her interaction with Jody, though she feigned interest in a magazine.

"Carey, look at my house now. Do you like it?" Jody asked.

"Very good, Jody. Keep it up, and soon you'll learn how to decorate as beautifully as your grandmother.

You have a very lovely home here, Mrs. Hensley." Carey wanted to draw Alex's mother into their conversation.

"Why, thank you, Carey." Mrs. Hensley slowly lowered her magazine, then set it aside and removed her reading glasses, letting them dangle from the gold chain about her neck.

"Even with a dollhouse like Jody's, you probably know lots of tricks about decorating and furniture arrangement." Carey's comment enticed Mrs. Hensley to slide from her velvet covered chair and join them on the floor. The older woman eyed critically the tiny dining room and parlor on the first floor of Jody's house.

"Victorian is hardly my forté, but a few minor changes might increase the living space here," she said, skillfully moving a piece at a time, explaining the reasons for doing so as she went along.

Carey's small encouragement was all Mrs. Hensley needed, and Carey excused herself, leaving grandmother and granddaughter alone together.

Carey found Jenine in the kitchen boning the turkey and occasionally popping juicy morsels into her mouth as she worked.

"Leftover turkey. I think it's my favorite. How about you, Carey? Would you like to take some home with you?" Jenine asked between bites.

"Thanks, I'd love a few slices." Carey adored cold turkey sandwiches, but she knew Jenine's family could easily polish off the leftovers without any help.

"Jenine," Carey spoke quietly. "You started to tell me why it had been so long since Alex brought a girlfriend home to meet his mother."

Jenine opened her mouth to reply, but a commotion outside the kitchen window caught her attention.

"Well, what do you know. They're back."

Three snowmen tromped through the side yard and

entered the back door, which opened onto a landing between the kitchen and basement.

Jenine quickly grabbed a broom from a small pantry closet and met them. "Back outside. All of you," she ordered like a drill sergeant, handing Ben the broom.

A few minutes later, they came inside again. From the kitchen, Carey listened to the teasing and laughter as Ben, Alex, and Scotty changed into dry clothes in the basement.

"Time for a fire in the fireplace," Alex announced, placing his cold hands on Carey's waist, holding her solidly by his side as they moved into the living room. He seated her on the sofa while he built a fire.

Mrs. Hensley and Jody had moved to an easy chair where the child curled in her grandmother's lap listening to an animated reading of the Christmas Mouse story. How much softer were Mrs. Hensley's features, Carey mused.

"Come on," Alex whispered, dragging her from the sofa. "I want to show you something while the fire kindles."

In the bedroom wing, Alex ushered her into a room filled with light. Shelves high and low held plants, some in flower, others simply green foliage. The entire room contained nothing but plant lights and plants.

"Heliconias?" Carey timidly asked.

Pride beamed across Alex's face. "I've been cross-pollinating them for years. One of these days, I'm going to come up with a variety I can patent and sell to the commercial markets. I'm getting closer all the time." Alex poured water from a jug into a watering can and automatically checked for dry specimens as he moved around the room.

"This is…" Carey searched for the right word, "incredible, Alex. You've really dedicated yourself to this, haven't you?"

"Absolutely. Of course, it would be easier in Florida, where most of the growers are located. I'd have closer access to market information, and I'd be on the cutting edge of the industry. It's tough, tucked away in the North, but this has always been my home. I'm not even sure I could leave if I wanted to," he paused, "I mean, with Mother here and all."

"You really have a big collection of plants between the college greenhouse, your apartment, and," she swept her hand out in front of her, "these."

"I like to spread them out, for security," Alex explained, returning the empty watering can to its place beside the jug. "A power outage or fire could occur anywhere. One disaster could wipe out years of effort. So for insurance, I keep some of my best specimens at each location."

As Alex spoke his gaze traveled over Carey's face and searched her eyes. He moved closer so his lips could brush against her forehead. Carey rested her cheek comfortably against Alex's shoulder. The thudding of his heartbeat, strong and quickened, warned her that Alex's response to their affection outpaced hers.

"I bet the fire's ready," she murmured, slipping out of his arms and pulling him toward the door.

Unexpectedly, he snatched her back. An almost imperceptible note of pleading swept across his features as he pressed her to him. Then he silently relented, turning her toward the door.

Scotty sat, bundled in an afghan, huddling in front of the fire. "What's the matter? Not warmed up yet?" Carey asked, kneeling beside him.

"I'm frozen," Scotty stammered, his teeth chattering. "Uncle Alex and Daddy and me made a snow fort. But the roof fell down on me. Lots of snow went down my neck."

Alex joined them, his grin turning into a chuckle. "He just giggled and laughed the whole time even when he was half buried in the snow."

"Did you really have fun doing all that?" Carey asked, rubbing one of Scotty's clammy feet between her hands while Alex massaged his back.

"It was great! I wish you had come, Carey. We slid down the hill a lot, too! I even pushed Daddy off the toboggan once."

"With some help from your uncle, huh, bruiser?" Alex added.

The warmth and flickering light of the fire cast a calm, relaxing spell over the living room. Ben reclined in an easy chair, feet up, puffing his pipe as he read a magazine. Mrs. Hensley and Jody dozed in the pink velvet winged chair, and Jenine curled on the end of the couch, entranced in the latest suspense novel by her favorite author.

What a lucky woman she is, Carey thought, hoping someday to have a family of her own as lovely as Jenine's. Alex seemed perfectly suited for fatherhood, bantering easily with either Scotty or Jody, guiding their behavior with gentle admonishment when necessary.

But Carey felt the prospect of having her own family remained far in the future. Her energies would be devoted for some time to keeping her family's business alive. Silently, she sighed. *All things work together for good*, she reminded herself, *and the Lord will work out His plan for me with His own divine timing.*

Chapter Five

"After the first of the year, eight hours of work a day. No more. I'm warning you, Carey, you'll be right back where you started," came the terse caution from Dr. Thompson. Then a grin cracked his solemn features. "I'm very pleased with your recovery. Now get dressed and get out of here, and remember what I said."

"Thanks Dr. Thompson. I'll follow your advice, I promise." Carey crossed her heart with her fingers as she had done as a kid when her mother made her agree to take bitter medicine without complaining.

Carey looked forward to working at the shop once again. She had recovered sufficiently to make resting at home a boring proposition.

After she returned home, Carey spent the rest of the day preparing for Todd and Amy's arrival. She expected her brother and his guest to arrive the next day on New Year's Eve.

Alex was coming over for a quiet private celebration, and she looked forward to his company. During the past week, he had spent a good deal of time at his mother's, and Carey realized she had missed him. He embodied so many fine qualities, Carey reasoned, but for now, it was enough to share his friendship. Anything else would come later.

The following afternoon, Carey heard the door open as she put the finishing touches on her tray of hors d'oeuvres. She ran to the entryway to meet her brother and his girlfriend.

"It's been a long time, little brother." Carey stood on tiptoe to kiss Todd on the cheek. Todd's build, like Carey's, was tall and slender, with about six inches more in height.

"Sis, this is Amy Warner. Amy, my 'big' sister, Carey." Todd scooted his little blonde companion in front of him, resting his hands on her shoulders.

"I'm thrilled to meet you, at last." Carey's out-stretched hand was met with Amy's limp, cold grip.

"We have some news for Carey, don't we, Amy? We're officially engaged." Todd proudly held out Amy's left hand. On her ring finger sat the biggest diamond Carey thought she had ever seen. She struggled to keep from gaping at it.

"Congratulations, you two. When's the wedding?" Carey finally managed to respond.

"Sometime this summer, I would imagine," Amy responded coolly. "Mummy and Daddy would simply die if we didn't wait until warm weather. They plan a huge garden party for the reception. It just wouldn't do to disappoint them, right Todd-honey?" Amy pinched Todd's cheek.

"That's an absolutely magnificent engagement ring, Amy," Carey commented, choosing her words carefully.

"Thank you. Your brother picked it out. He didn't give me much choice in the matter. Todd said I'd have to trust his judgment." She watched the diamond glimmer as she tilted her hand in the natural light from the front picture window.

It wasn't the most brilliant stone Carey had ever laid eyes on, but she was sure it weighed at least a karat. How could Todd afford such a ring? She put these thoughts aside for the time being and attended to her guest's needs.

"I'll show you your room, Amy, whenever you're ready to unpack."

"Good idea, Sis." Todd broke in. "While you two get to know each other, I'm going to run down to the store to pick up some supplies for tonight. Hey, what are these?" Todd asked, stealing a cheese and olive-topped cracker from Carey's painstakingly prepared tray.

"Cut it out, Todd," Carey warned, snatching the tray from the dining table. "These are for tonight."

"I'll be back soon, pumpkin-face," Todd teased, kissing Amy's forehead.

Carey showed Amy the guest bedroom and where her towels were hanging in the bathroom, then left her to freshen up.

In the kitchen, Carey prepared carrot and celery sticks, radishes, broccoli, and cauliflower to go with vegetable dip. A few minutes later, Amy joined her at the kitchen table.

"Todd and I drove around the area a bit before coming here." Amy munched a carrot stick between words. "He showed me the mansion your folks had planned to buy just north of town. I mean, before their…accident."

"He did?" Carey masked her surprise and waited for Amy to continue.

"He said you hate being alone in a big house and wanted to be within walking distance of everything, so you decided not to carry through your parents' plans to buy the mansion. It's really kind of cozy and quaint here." She scanned the kitchen in mock appreciation.

"And Todd said you have plans to remodel the place inside and out."

"What else did Todd tell you?" Carey asked hesitantly, afraid of the answer.

"Not very much, really. He's pretty tight-lipped about your parents' investments. You'd never know he just inherited a fortune. He's quite humble about the whole thing."

"I can imagine," Carey responded flatly, wondering what other false notions Todd had planted in Amy's head. Carey resolved to confront Todd alone at the first opportunity.

"Mind if I watch TV?" Amy asked, wandering into the living room. She snapped on the set without waiting for an answer.

"The listing is on the table next to the recliner," Carey offered, continuing to prepare the vegetables at the kitchen table.

The front door swung open a few minutes later. "Hey Amy, get set for a big night on the town. I've got enough here for one huge celebration," Todd announced, setting a large grocery bag on the dining table. "How long will it take you to get ready?"

"An hour, at least. Maybe more, since I'm meeting all your buddies at the party tonight." Amy fluttered her eyelashes lazily. "I've got to look especially terrific for my man," she drawled, pulling herself up on tiptoe for a kiss.

"Better get started then. You have to rough it in this house. It's a one-bathroom operation." Todd sent Amy down the hall with a playful swat to her behind.

Carey approached Todd as he removed the contents of his sack. "You lied to her, Todd."

A momentary look of discomfort crossed his face, then the corner of his mouth twisted in a calculating

60

grin. "Now, Sis, don't be angry with me."

"Todd, you're just complicating matters between yourself and Amy with your lies. You have to tell her the truth, or she'll surely learn it from someone else."

"You wouldn't." His words were half-statement, half-question.

Carey waited to respond. "You're right. I wouldn't. At least not until I give you the chance to tell her yourself. Promise me, Todd, you'll tell her the truth. We're not wealthy. We're not even well off. You need to tell her that." Carey's volume rose, her plea mixing anger with desperation.

"Just give me tonight," Todd begged. "Then I promise I'll come clean with Amy. I said things about Mom and Dad having money tied up in investments only to impress her. Believe me, I'll take care of it tonight."

Carey's head moved slowly from side to side. "I don't know why I should believe you. After all the lies you told her, you're probably lying to me, too." She turned and walked away, then swung around. "Another thing. Where did you get the money for that diamond ring?"

Todd darted a look at his watch and fumbled with his jacket zipper. "Look, I haven't even stopped by the shop to say hello to the Emerys. It's almost closing time."

"Todd, where did the money come from? Answer me," she challenged.

An impish smile spread across his features, giving him a boyishly innocent appeal. "Come on, Sis, a fellow doesn't give away all his secrets. That's part of the intrigue of romance." Todd slipped out the door before Carey could say more.

Todd and Amy left for their dinner party and New Year's celebration before Carey could corner Todd again to ask him about Amy's ring.

With just a half hour before Alex's arrival, she had the house to herself again. Amy had monopolized the bathroom for nearly two hours. Now Carey frantically showered and changed, applying the last of her makeup as the doorbell rang.

Carey and Alex spent a quiet evening watching New Year's festivities on television. It ended soon after they watched the ball drop in New York City's Times Square.

When Carey awoke late the next morning, Todd and Amy still had not returned. Assuming their celebration had gone on longer than expected, Carey fixed brunch for herself and flicked on the television. Her mind, however drifted to her conversation with Alex the night before.

"Did you speak with Todd about helping more at the shop?"

"Not yet."

"When are you going to talk to him about it?"

"Soon, Alex. It's hard to pin him down. I'll talk to him before he leaves. I promise."

"You'd better. I'd hate to see you sick all over again the next time a rush comes along. At Easter, for instance."

"I'll make him help out. You'll see."

Alone, Carey watched the New Year's Day Parade and part of the first football game scheduled for the afternoon. Finally, the front door opened, and a bedraggled Amy and Todd shuffled in.

"I'm hitting the sack, Sis. It's been a tough night, hasn't it, pumpkin-face?"

Amy nodded. "Let's get some sleep. We've got to drive back to school tonight."

"Can I get either of you anything?" Carey offered.

Todd had already gone down the hall without responding.

"No thanks, Carey," Amy replied. "Guess I'll nap for a bit, too." She placed her coat over a dining chair and disappeared into her room.

Several hours passed without a stir. Finally, a little after eight o'clock that evening, Carey heard Amy knock on Todd's bedroom door to awaken him. Thirty minutes later, they stood at the front door.

"We've got to hit the road for Cornell, Sis. It will be almost midnight before we get back, as it is." Todd gripped his bag and wedged Amy's above it under his arm.

"Can I get you anything before you go?" Carey offered. "Sandwiches or a thermos of coffee?"

"Aspirin. I could use a couple of aspirin," Todd answered.

Carey found a small bottle in the medicine cabinet and tucked it into Todd's jacket pocket. "Drive carefully, and if you get sleepy, stop and rest."

"I'll keep him awake," Amy volunteered, "and thanks for the hospitality, Carey. You've got a nice cozy little bungalow here."

"You're welcome, Amy. Come again soon, whenever you and Todd can."

"Sure thing, Sis. Come on, Amy, we've got to get a move on."

Carey watched as Todd backed out of the driveway. She couldn't decide whether the lack of opportunity to confront Todd about upholding his responsibility for the greenhouse had resulted from Todd's devious planning or from happenstance. In either case, the result was the same. She could not count on Todd for help with the business in the near future. Nor had she uncovered any information about Todd's purchase of Amy's diamond.

As Carey went to bed that night, her brother's situation churned in her mind. Finally, after an hour or more, she drifted into a light, restless sleep.

Her alarm went off earlier than she was accustomed to. Carey dressed and applied plenty of blusher as she put on her makeup. She slipped on a fuzzy pink sweater, hoping it would bring out the color in her cheeks. It wouldn't do to have Maggie telling her she looked pale on her first day back to work.

Carey arrived at the shop before the Emerys did and immediately turned up the thermostat in the office, then filled and plugged in the coffeepot. She twisted the knob on the safe and extracted the bag containing change and bills for the cash register. She puzzled momentarily over an unmarked white envelope, slit open at one end and stuffed fat with bills, then remembered it was payment for Jack Brothers roses. Carey filled the compartments of the cash register drawer and tossed the white envelope beneath the tray. She had just finished when Maggie and Floyd pulled into the driveway.

"There she is, looking just like summer sunshine," Maggie called as she stepped through the side door of the shop.

"Glad to see your color back, Carey," Floyd added. "I must say, it's a big improvement over the last time I saw you."

"It's nice to be back to normal. I started going crazy, sitting around the house." Carey slipped her arm around Maggie's ample waist and squeezed the grandmotherly friend, then kissed Floyd on the cheek.

"If you don't mind my recommendation, you might just sit around here some and tend to those billings." Maggie pointed out a stack of paperwork piled on the desk. "There are plenty of invoices to send out, and the sooner the better."

"I get the hint. You'd rather do anything but paperwork. Right?" Carey eased into a smile. "I'll start on it just as soon as I take a look out back."

Carey followed Floyd to the greenhouses, noting the unsold poinsettias. Happily, only a few of the traditional Christmas plants remained on the benches. What was left would be sold at discount within a day or two. As she had promised Maggie, she returned to the office and worked diligently on billings while Maggie waited on customers and answered phone calls.

Morning coffee break came and went, and the next time Carey looked up, it was to see Gavin Jack entering the side door. Her heart lurched. In his familiar black leather jacket, black pants, and cap, he created a formidable image.

For a split second, his dark, mysterious eyes rested on her, then the tall, dark figure carried a heavy pail of roses to the cooler. Carey watched the powerful man move with an easy grace.

Her pulse quickened. She had forgotten this was Gavin's regular delivery day. Her fingers trembled as she sealed a bill inside an envelope, and she felt completely speechless. Thankfully, Maggie had gone to the back storage room for some planters, and couldn't witness her reaction to Gavin's presence.

Then, like lightning, the thought struck her that she still owed him payment. Carey swiftly retrieved the white envelope from the cash register. When Gavin returned from the cooler, she held it out to him without explanation.

He looked at her with cool regard, his dark irises moving lazily over her, assessing her thoroughly. Seconds stretched interminably, it seemed, before Gavin took the envelope from her. Leaning against the side counter, he blew into the slit end. Gavin eyed its contents, then spoke at last.

"The holiday was profitable, I trust?" His quiet words belied the tension between them.

Carey nodded, begging her voice to return.

"Good." Gavin moved the wad of bills from the envelope and placed them in his leather money clip. "This your first day back?" he asked, smiling as he wadded the envelope into a tight little ball, then propelled it neatly into the basket beneath the customer counter behind her.

"Yes. Yes, it is," she haltingly replied.

"Since your holiday was profitable, and this is your first day back," he continued, ignoring her uneasiness, "I'll treat you to lunch." His voice was low and smooth. "And I've noticed," he added deliberately, "that not all of those roses I brought you faded away."

"What are you talking about?" She clipped off the words without thinking.

"You must have half a dozen of them right there in your cheeks." Without trying, Gavin had caused a wave of scarlet to flow from her neck to her forehead. A boyish smile took over his features, then he added, "Now stop blushing and get your coat."

Disturbed by Gavin's easy confidence in her response, Carey spoke defiantly. "I haven't yet agreed to have lunch with you, Gavin Jack." She paused then, realizing how tempting the prospect was, and warned herself to push such feelings aside. "Besides," she continued, "it's way too early."

"It is?" He eyed the clock above her head.

One glance told Carey she had lost all track of time. She'd been doubly thrown by the timing of Gavin's delivery. He usually arrived about midmorning. It was now past noon.

66

Maggie returned from the storage room with an armload of ceramic planters. "Carey, what are you doing here? It's lunch time, don't you know?" She paused to set the planters on a table, then looked curiously at Gavin.

Gavin nodded, and Maggie nodded back. Flustered, Carey retrieved her coat from its peg. Maggie always waited for Carey to return from lunch before taking a break herself. Now Carey had made Maggie's wait that much longer.

"I'm sorry, Maggie. I didn't even notice the time. My mind was on other things, I guess. I won't be gone long." Carey grabbed her handbag and brushed past Gavin. "I'll see you in a while, then, Maggie."

Carey stepped out the side door, followed closely by Gavin, who hooked his arm in hers. Her heart hammered as he fell into step beside her.

"I'd like to know, Carey, why it's such a horrible fate, having lunch with me?"

"All right, Gavin. I'll have lunch with you. But understand from the start, it's strictly business."

Gavin helped her into his van, half lifting her with his strong, large hands about her waist. His touch had a powerful effect on her, one she wished to ignore, yet found she couldn't suppress.

Without a word of explanation Gavin drove out of Stockport. Nervously, Carey wondered if she'd made a mistake. She knew of no restaurants on the road he'd taken, and she really knew very little about Gavin Jack.

A few miles south of town, off to the side of a narrow country road, Gavin pulled up in front of a concrete-block structure with a sign reading Polly's Place. Two cars were parked in front—hardly the sign of a popular eatery at the peak of a lunch hour.

Her regrets surfaced as Carey looked at the squat

building and imagined the dark, dingy interior—the bare tables, dirty floor, smell of burned grease, and barroom conversation.

Gavin helped her from the van, his arm about her waist as he walked her to the door. She told herself he did so only to help her across the slippery surface of the parking area, but this contact sent tingles through her veins, nonetheless.

Posted on the front door, a sign clearly marked the business CLOSED. Ignoring it, Gavin yanked open the warped door and motioned her inside.

"Everything's ready, Gavin," an elderly plump woman sang out as the door closed behind them. The interior, fresh and bright as a spring day, totally belied the outward appearance of Polly's Place.

"Polly, come over here for a minute. I want you to meet someone." Gavin helped Carey out of her coat, hanging it on a coat tree near the door. While the large woman made her way to them, winding between the tables, Gavin removed his jacket and hung it next to Carey's coat.

"Carey, this is Polly. Polly, Carey McIlwain."

"Carey, I'm pleased to have you here. Gavin's told me a little about you. I hope you're over that pneumonia." Polly enfolded Carey's hand in her fat-padded ones.

"Pronounced healthy by my family doctor. Thank you for your concern."

Polly looked at her critically. "My, but you do look like you could use some meat on those bones. Hope you like chicken and biscuits, because that's what Gavin ordered. Pick your spot, and I'll be right out." Polly left for the kitchen.

"You heard the lady. Pick your spot," Gavin urged.

Carey scanned the small but immaculate room and led Gavin to a corner booth only large enough for two, on the opposite end of the room from the kitchen. She slid into one side of the booth and Gavin slid in opposite her.

With a quick assessment of her surroundings, Carey noticed that all of the tables and chairs were made of natural oak, not the cheap chrome and plastic common in so many diners. Thick, sapphire-blue pads covered the oak seats of both the chairs and booth benches, and matching blue placemats and napkins decorated the tables.

When Carey's eyes returned to Gavin she realized he had been watching her closely. The beginning of a smile tipped the corners of his mouth.

"Now, you see, it's not what you expected, is it, Carey?"

"What do you mean?"

"Come on, Carey. I'd have to be blind to miss the worried look all over your face when I pulled up out front."

Before she could deny the truth, Polly approached their table carrying a tray laden with piping hot plates of biscuits smothered in chicken and gravy. The hearty aroma was delicious enough to make Carey's stomach grumble.

"Need anything else?" she asked, setting the pot of coffee between them.

"All set, Polly. Thanks," Gavin answered.

Carey took a small bite of the steaming serving. Its taste lived up to its aroma. Words seemed unnecessary as she and Gavin enjoyed the first few bites, then he broke the silence.

"You know, Carey, that plant doctor from the college,...what's his name?"

"Hensley," Carey said, "Doctor Alex Hensley. What about him?"

69

"I hope you realize he's too old for you. Besides," his lips twisted into a smile, "he's way too stuffy."

"Is that what you brought me here to tell me?" she demanded, yet knowing she sounded unreasonably defensive. "You could have saved yourself all the trouble, Gavin Jack, because I don't need or appreciate your comments about my friends."

Flustered, Carey jabbed her fork at the food on her plate, determined not to play a game of semantics. But in reflection, he'd made a comment she knew she couldn't ignore. Unless her judgment was grossly lacking, Gavin and Alex were nearly identical in age. She couldn't resist the temptation to pursue the issue.

"You bear the same fault Alex does," she asserted. "I would guess you're the same age as Alex Hensley within a year or so. So how can you accuse him of being too old?" She leaned back with an air of self-confidence.

"Simple," Gavin replied. "Age is a mental attitude. He's already over the hill."

"If it's mental attitude that determines maturity, then you're still a juvenile," she taunted, but immediately regretted the remark.

A strained silence ensued, during which time Carey had ample opportunity to wonder why Gavin had even asked her to lunch. But another more superficial circumstance raised her curiosity, and she mentioned it as a means of reopening communication.

"Why were you so late with your deliveries this morning, Gavin? Usually, you're through Stockport a couple of hours earlier." She waited for his explanation while he helped himself to more chicken. Half listening, she expected to hear one of the usual reasons—his van stalled; he got a late start. In no way was she prepared for the words he spoke next.

"It was the only way I could think of to convince you to eat lunch with me."

Startled, Carey stopped chewing, unsure how to react.

"Of course, I prefer a pretty face to an empty booth when I eat here," Gavin explained nonchalantly, "and since Polly already planned on me for lunch, I just figured I'd have her cook up a double helping."

"You could have just invited me to lunch in the normal fashion, without using all this pretense." Her words were soft. "I didn't realize I was so unapproachable."

Gavin's hand covered hers. "You're anything but—I was just…" His eyes searched hers for understanding.

"Afraid I'd turn you down?" she finished for him.

Gavin nodded and withdrew his hand. "I have a bad habit of scaring people off. I thought I'd done the same to you."

"You do come on pretty strong sometimes, like the night the furnace broke down. I thought you were going to break the door in." Carey chuckled at the memory, then her expression grew more serious. "I really appreciated your helping me save my poinsettias. At the time, I was too angry with your interference to tell you. Thanks, Gavin."

Gavin's dark eyes softened, and the corners of his mouth pulled into a slight smile. "I was glad to help out."

A question formed in Carey's mind as she savored another mouthful of chicken. "Gavin, how did you find out about this place," she wondered, her eyes sweeping the room. "Polly's a wonderful cook. You must have some charm, to get the whole restaurant to yourself."

Gavin's brows arched as he cast a mischievous look her way. "I'll tell you this much. I haven't met a woman yet who could resist roses."

Carey grinned. Gavin knew his strong points all too well.

A few moments later, Polly came through the swinging kitchen doors carrying a tray laden with desserts. "Ready for your dessert, dears? We have homemade pie, cakes, fresh chocolate e'clairs. How about a piece of my mountain lemon pie?" she asked, indicating the pieces with the two-inch-high meringue topping.

"Polly's lemon pie is the best, Carey. I'm going to have some. Why don't you?"

"I really shouldn't, but I can't resist," Carey admitted, eyeing the mouth-watering pie.

When Gavin had taken a few bites of his pie, he looked at Carey thoughtfully. "I wanted to ask you a question."

He paused to heighten the effect.

"Are you sure you're going to be happy in the florist business? I think it's a shame you've given up on teaching."

Gavin's question took her completely by surprise. Eventually, she responded very honestly. "I loved my teaching job, but my responsibility for my family's business comes first."

"So it's just that simple?" Gavin asked, shaking his head slowly from side to side.

"Yes, it is. In spite of your disbelief," Carey solemnly stated.

They said little else as they finished their dessert.

Carey watched curiously as Gavin extracted his money clip from his rear pocket. Polly had presented him with no check, but Gavin slipped several bills, the very ones she'd paid him earlier that day, from the clip and placed them on the center of the table.

Silence filled Gavin's van most of the way back to Stockport. Carey wondered why, instead of pulling into the greenhouse driveway, Gavin pulled up in front of her house. Before she could ask any questions, he had jumped out and opened the rear door of the van. A moment later, he opened her door.

"Let's find a place for these inside before I take you back to work," he said, offering her a bouquet of two dozen roses in various colors.

"But Gavin, why?" She paused to inhale their delicate fragrance.

"Just because I want you to have them."

Just because I want you to have them. The words echoed in Carey's mind as she tried to concentrate on her billing work while Maggie and Floyd were out to lunch. Fortunately, the job didn't require a lot of concentration, because her throughts returned to Gavin again and again.

The thought which troubled her most was his concern that she had given up on teaching. Perhaps he would never understand her reason for doing so. Or did he know something about her she had not yet learned about herself?

Carey loved music, had loved her ten, eleven and twelve-year-old students, and was delighted when her training and experience enabled her to help others learn.

Aside from teaching music in the school, she had given several students private guitar lessons after hours. Since her return to Stockport, Carey had played her guitar during the opening of each Sunday school hour at church. During her recuperation period, she had played quite a bit just for her own enjoyment. In fact, perhaps more than anything else, increasing her time with her classical guitar had reminded her how much she missed teaching music.

Finally Carey laid her pen beside the high stack of sealed statements. Though she loved teaching she would have to put it aside in the year ahead. Her greatest desire was to put McIlwain Greenhouses solidly in the black. It was the toughest task she'd known.

Chapter Six

"Let's settle down, kids. What do you say? It's time to get started. Are you ready, Carey?" Pastor Mike, the assistant minister in charge of education, signaled her to start the first song at the opening of the Sunday school hour. All the classes, young and old, gathered in the large basement room for a few choruses of old favorites before going to smaller separate rooms to study their lessons.

This was a treat for Carey each Sunday. In addition to her love of instrumental music, she enjoyed singing to guitar accompaniment, especially when joined by the high voices of the four, five, and six-year-olds singing their favorites like, "Jesus Loves Me." The hand motions added interest to some songs, and often Pastor Mike would help her lead the group in singing rounds.

Today was her first day to play again since recovering from pneumonia. After the singing, several people stopped to say they had missed the guitar accompaniment during her illness. Carey felt good, knowing others appreciated her musical contribution.

"I got a guitar for Christmas, Carey," Sarah, an eight-year-old, said. Pastor Mike had dismissed the group to their Sunday school classrooms, and Carey put away her guitar and music.

"You did? Are you taking lessons?" Carey asked. It seemed a natural question.

"Not yet. Mommy's trying to find someone to teach me, but she hasn't found anyone yet." Sarah plucked the strings of Carey's guitar, then her eyes lit. "You could teach me, couldn't you, Carey?" Her voice rose with excitement.

Carey thought about her responsibilities at the shop, and her promise to Dr. Thompson not to work more than eight hours a day.

"Please, Carey. You could do it, if you only wanted to," Sarah pleaded.

"Sometimes it isn't a matter of what we want to do, Sarah, but rather what we have to do. I have other responsibilities besides music. I'd like to teach you, but I'll have to let you know. O.K.?"

Sarah's face dropped. "When will you know?"

"Soon. Now you'd better get going, or you'll be late to class."

All through Sunday school and church service, Carey dreamed what it would be like to teach again. Could she risk the time and energy it might take to give music lessons, when she had so newly recovered from her illness?

Carey prayed for guidance, and again and again she had the identical thought—teaching part-time was the perfect way to keep her hand in music while devoting her fulltime efforts to the florist shop.

After the church service, Carey sought out Sarah's mother. "Mrs. Campbell, Sarah says you're looking for someone to teach her guitar. I'd be glad to."

"Oh, Carey, would you, honestly?" Mrs. Campbell asked. "I thought about you, but knowing you had been so ill, I figured it would be too much to ask, in addition to your regular job."

"I'd enjoy it more than you know."

"Oh, goody," Sarah exclaimed, jumping up and down at her mother's side.

"That means you have to practice every day, Sarah," her mother warned her. "Carey doesn't want to spend her time with you unless you work hard."

"I'll practice. I promise. I've got to go tell Billy."

Mrs. Campbell watched Sarah skip away, then added, "If you're interested in more students, Billy and another boy might want lessons too. At least three in Sarah's class received guitars as Christmas gifts this year."

"If Saturday mornings would work out, I could take a small group," Carey explained.

"I'll have the other mothers get in touch with you."

"Thank you, Mrs. Campbell. I'd appreciate that."

January melded into February, and before Carey knew it, Valentine's Day had arrived. Extra orders poured in. She and Maggie rushed all day long to keep up with the constant ringing of the telephone and steady stream of walk-in customers.

After work, Carey plopped into her father's recliner to rest while she shuffled through her mail. At the bottom of the stack lay a large envelope bearing Alex Hensley's return address. Inside, she found a huge card with a pop-out heart and a note from Alex. "I wish I could be with you today, but family obligations prevented my seeing you. I'll call you soon for lunch. Fond regards, Alex."

Carey set the card on the television and relaxed again in the recliner. She thought back on the day, and the dozens of orders she'd filled for men who wanted to remember that special woman in their lives, and wondered about Gavin. Secretly, she wished he had sent her a card, but he just didn't seem the type.

She leaned her head back and closed her eyes. Eventually she'd find the energy to rummage in the refrigerator and prepare leftovers for dinner.

A knock on the door startled Carey, and she realized she had been asleep for quite some time. When she opened the door, Gavin smiled at her, his arms laden with packages.

"Happy Valentine's Day, Carey!" He stepped inside, setting a bag and two boxes on the dining table. "I tried to call all day long, but your greenhouse phone was tied up."

Astonished, Carey stared wordlessly as Gavin removed the cover from a long, narrow box. Deep red roses tied together with a huge satin bow stared back. She gasped when she saw them.

"Gavin, they're beautiful, thank you." Carey lifted the bouquet from the box and cradled them in her arms, burying her nose in the blossoms. When she looked into Gavin's face, she could see he was pleased at her response.

"I think you'd better get them into water right away," Gavin suggested. "They've been in that box for several hours."

Carey went to the kitchen to fill a vase with water. When she returned, he had cleared the dining table of all but a collection of white Styrofoam containers.

"I'll find a place for those," Gavin offered taking the roses, "if you could just rustle up some silverware. Polly sends her best, and I've got two helpings of her prime rib right here to prove it."

"I'll bet Polly's got roses tonight," Carey conjectured with a laugh. She returned with the silverware to find Gavin placing the vase of roses on the television, Alex's card folded and turned face down beside it. She smiled to herself.

Polly's prime rib was excellent, along with the baked potatoes, tossed salads, homemade dinner rolls, and mountain lemon pie.

"Gavin," Carey looked up at him, noting his handsome dark eyes, "Thank you for bringing dinner. It was very thoughtful of you." She laid her fork across her empty pie plate.

Gavin reached for her hand and squeezed it inside his large, strong ones before releasing it again. His tenderness sent a warm shiver through her.

"I wanted to see you tonight, but I knew you'd have a busy day at work and would be tired. Letting Polly pack us a dinner seemed like a good idea."

Gavin moved to clear the table and Carey helped, throwing empty food containers into a paper sack. She gathered her silverware and took it to the kitchen. When she returned, Gavin held out a heart-shaped box to her.

"I hope you saved just a little bit of room for one of these."

Carey looked at the red foil-covered box for a moment before opening it. "You're full of surprises tonight. Thank you," she managed, her voice shaky with emotion. She eased off the lid and tasted a chocolate cream, letting it melt on her tongue.

Gavin moved toward the door, pulling on his leather cap. "I'd better be going. I still have work to do. Good night, Carey."

"Good night, Gavin." Carey leaned against the open door and watched him go. As his taillights faded from view, she wondered about the tender side of Gavin Jack, the side buried beneath his tough leather jacket and cap.

The short days of winter followed one another in routine fasion, turning eventually into weeks, and lengthening gradually with the coming of a new season.

Carey saw Alex perhaps once a week. Their relationship felt comfortable. Generally, they shared a lunch together or some college activity such as a play or concert. Occasionally, they babysat for Scotty and Jody.

By late winter, Gavin had made several more deliveries, but had not asked Carey out, nor displayed interest in engaging in any lengthy conversations since their dinner together on Valentine's Day. His aloofness puzzled her, especially when she could point to incidents that proved him to be sensitive and caring—the fruitbasket left on her doorstep after her parents' deaths, his help with the furnace, the bouquet of roses during her illness, and more recently, the lunch they'd shared at Polly's and his Valentine's Day surprises.

As the weeks went by, Carey noticed a gradual softening in his image. He had traded his tough-looking, black leather jacket for a cobalt blue jacket of a similar style, but fashioned from fabric. Beneath the partially opened zipper, Carey saw that a dark shirt and a tie in a muted pattern had replaced his ribbed sweater.

Gavin's hair was now carefully trimmed and styled, losing the tousled, wet look of earlier times, and his clean-shaven face lacked the stubbly growth he had sometimes allowed. His cap, the distressed leather knickerbocker relic, had disappeared entirely.

One Wednesday morning in late February, Carey had backed the greenhouse truck into the area of the driveway usually kept clear for vendors' deliveries. She intended to unload some office supplies, but a few minutes before Gavin's usual arrival time, she was unable to start the truck.

With some effort, she raised the truck's hood. Carey

possessed a limited knowledge of auto mechanics, but she soon located the distributor cap and loosened it, thinking the problem might be there. She heard Gavin's truck pull up, and motioned him to park out front, several yards from the side door of the shop.

When Gavin approached the greenhouse lugging his heavy pail of roses, Carey buried her head under the hood. She waited for Gavin to comment as he squeezed between the greenhouse truck and the building, headed for the side door.

"Problems, Carey?" Gavin plunked the rose pail on the small patch of driveway between the truck and the door. The bright winter sunshine, intensified by its reflection off the white ground cover, outlined the handsome smoothness of Gavin's cheek and jawbone.

She looked up into his obsidian eyes and tried to ignore the erratic rhythm of her heart. "Gavin. I'm sorry for the inconvenience. She stalled on me right here, and I can't seem to get her started again." His fresh cleanness and the fragrance of the roses mingled with the clear cold February air and tingled in her nostrils. His shoulder rubbed against hers as he leaned under the hood.

Gavin eyed the engine skeptically, then straightened, cocking one brow at her. "Let me get these inside before they freeze." He hefted the pail of roses from the ground. "Then I'll take another look."

Carey felt both weak and excited as Gavin disappeared through the door. Weeks had passed since she had eaten lunch with him at Polly's, and Carey had told herself that Gavin's quiet reserve, in the interim, hadn't bothered her. She couldn't possibly feel something for a man who kept his thoughts and feelings so locked inside. Now, within a few short moments, he had proven her wrong.

A minute later, Gavin returned. "I suppose it won't hurt to check this, but I doubt the trouble is in the distributor." He then inspected the battery terminals. He wiped them clean, and cleaned the connections. "That might have been the problem. Let me see your keys."

Carey felt in her pockets. With increasing discomfort, she remembered hanging them on their hook in the shop after backing the truck to its present, inconvenient location.

"I must have left them inside after I discovered it wouldn't start. Just a second." Carey dashed inside and grabbed the keys from their hook, pausing long enough to wonder how she would ease the conversation into more personal topics. She would have to depend on pure intuition, she concluded, as she returned to Gavin.

"I think the dirty terminals were the problem." Gavin didn't bother looking up as he spoke. His long, strong fingers pressed against the battery cables to reconnect them. "You might consider getting a new battery. This one's seen better days." His look of concern and interest pleased Carey. "I'll try to start it now."

She dropped the keys into his outstretched hand. In a single motion of grace and agility, Gavin swung himself up into the driver's seat. Instantly, the truck fired up. He left the engine idling while he closed the hood.

"How can I ever thank you?" Carey asked, moving beside him in the cramped space between the truck and the flower shop. "It might have cost me a fortune in repair bills at a garage."

He stepped back, putting some distance between them. "Carey, when will you ever learn?" A thread of mock annoyance laced his tone.

"What's that supposed to mean?" She bit her lower lip, and made a feeble attempt to smile. All the while her mind spun crazily in search of a way to prolong their encounter.

"I've got to give you credit, Carey. You've outlasted my predictions in keeping the business afloat, but you've got a long way to go." Gavin combed his fingers through his dark, thick hair, shook his head in exasperation, and moved toward his truck.

"Have you seen Polly lately?" It was a last-ditch effort. With her truck still running, she didn't have much time to penetrate the aloofness which seemed to accompany his new smoother image.

He wasted neither time nor energy for a verbal reply, but shook his head as he climbed back into his truck. Raising his hand in a parting gesture, he pulled out into traffic and disappeared from view.

Carey climbed into her own truck, pulled it forward in the driveway, and shut it off. Resignedly, she yanked the keys from the ignition. Gavin appeared more remote than ever. She must banish all thoughts and feelings for him from her mind. Today's encounter proved that she was not the person to draw out Gavin Jack.

Nevertheless, the image of his strong lean form crept forward in her mind, along with rememberance of the crisp clean fragrance of his cologne. These memories, along with humiliation over her unsuccessful attempt to draw him into conversation made her face burn. Carey waited for the color to drain from her cheeks, then went inside.

"Everything all right?" Maggie asked the moment Carey stepped into the shop.

"Fine, Maggie." Carey's voice held a listless, empty quality she didn't intend.

"You're sure? What was all that about the truck?" Maggie's concern sounded like prying and only grated on Carey's nerves.

Carey unwrapped her fuzzy blue scarf, the one Alex

had given her for Christmas, and pulled off her mittens, before answering. "Nothing at all. Just a little problem with the battery," Carey said, a little too briskly.

"Just checking. Didn't mean to pry." Maggie clipped off the words. Quickly, she resumed work on a flower arrangement.

Carey hung her coat and stepped into the restroom to comb her hair. A sour image stared back at her from the bathroom mirror. "You certainly look unhappy today. No wonder you're running into problems," she told herself, smoothing several long auburn strands into place behind her ear.

Carey dug into her handbag and found her lip gloss. Perhaps a bit of outward color would help her spirits. The new layer of gloss in place, Carey practiced moving the corners of her mouth upward. A silly ritual, she thought at first, but in a few seconds, she felt better about herself and went straight to Maggie's side.

"Please forgive my earlier bad mood. I promise to improve for the rest of the day."

Maggie went on working almost as if she hadn't heard Carey speak. But gradually, though she didn't look up, her mouth curved into a grin. Then she dropped her work and hugged Carey to her side.

"You're entitled to your bad moods like anyone else."

The phone rang, and Maggie released Carrey. "Why don't you answer that for dear old Maggie? I've got to finish this before the customer comes back and discovers his belated anniversary gift will be even later."

Carey picked up the extension in the front of the shop, rather than the one next to Maggie's arranging table, and as soon as she heard the voice on the other end, she was glad she had.

"Alex. I'm so glad you called....Lunch sounds great. See you shortly after twelve. Bye."

Chapter Seven

Carey checked her list once again: florist's foil, acetate ribbon, florist's picks, green tape, helium balloons, corsage pins, Styrofoam sheets, hanging baskets, rooting trays, and bud vases. She hoped Robinson's Supply in Rochester would have everything in stock.

"I'm on my way, Maggie. Can you think of anything else?"

Maggie set aside the corsage she was working on and read the list. "Guess not. Looks like a beautiful day, all sunshiny and bright for a change. March weather isn't all bad, 'specially toward the end of the month. But you be careful just the same. Rochester traffic can be awful, and there might still be some slippery patches on the road."

"Got it. See you later." Carey shoved the list into her pocket and shouldered her bag.

The drive toward Rochester brought memories of her parents and reenforced in her mind Maggie's wise admonition—to drive carefully. Five long months had passed since Patrick and Helen McIlwain had met their fate on the road from Rochester to Stockport.

Carey switched on the truck radio, determined to repress the painful memory. She sang with the radio and forced her mind onto more pleasant topics. About twenty minutes later, she dug the scrap of paper from her coat pocket bearing Floyd's crude map.

Following his instructions carefully, she turned down a narrow country road. A few miles later, the landscape grew vaguely familiar. A large white sign with red lettering loomed in front of her: "Jack Brothers Roses, Next Right."

She remembered now visiting Jack Brothers years ago with her father. Carey wondered if the place had changed much. She considered stopping by, then dismissed the idea as unwise. Still, it was right on her way. Her curiosity overcame her hesitation when she approached the entrance. As if self-directed, the greenhouse van turned into the Jack Brothers Roses driveway.

Suddenly, her heart raced. Would she run into Gavin, or was he out making deliveries? What would she say if she saw him?

Several greenhouses strung one after the other jutted off to her left. Straight ahead stood a tiny office building. Carey stopped her van and stepped out. As she neared the office, she caught a glimpse of a large, white home set on a small rise in the distance to her right. Its large, circular drive brought *The Great Gatsby* to mind, especially with the low-slung sportscar parked directly in front.

Whether or not Jack Brothers Roses included the residence, Carey couldn't tell. She didn't remember seeing it as a child, but that was many years ago and things could have changed since then.

Gavin's delivery van wasn't in sight, and she heaved a sigh of relief. Carey stepped briskly inside the office door. Its small, but expensively furnished, interior included space enough for two chairs and a desk occupied by a very young and pretty, dark-haired receptionist—Darleen Williams, according to her nameplate. Darleen smiled up at her.

"I'm Carey McIlwain, McIlwain Greenhouses, Stockport. Jack Brothers supplies my roses. I was driving through the area and thought I'd stop for a quick tour. Could I take a walk through the greenhouses?"

"I'll call one of our employees to guide you," Darleen offered, lifting her phone.

Gavin stepped into the room from a door at the back, the power of his presence bordering on intimidation. "That won't be necessary, Darleen. I'll escort Miss McIlwain myself," he said smoothly, with no expression of surprise at seeing Carey.

Carey's heart lurched. "Hello, Gavin." Her voice faltered as she made a weak attempt to smile.

Wordlessly, he waited for her to pass in front of him through the narrow door leading from the receptionist's office. As she brushed past him, she was aware that his dark eyes never left her.

Gavin led her through the employee lounge where several men and two young women in coveralls were eating at small tables. A glance at the wall clock told Carey her timing was bad. It was a few minutes past noon.

"I came here once when I was little," Carey explained awkwardly. "My father brought me along for the ride, more than anything, I guess." She spoke nervously, hoping to reduce the tension she sensed between them.

Gavin remained quiet. They walked outside between buildings. He held open the door to the first greenhouse. Three rows of benches stretched before them, at least a hundred feet in all. As the door came to rest against its jamb, a tattered, yellow page hanging there caught her eye. She stepped closer to read its faded lettering.

Silent Partner

For the love of roses, we began.

Toil and dedication brought success, financial reward
—then an arrogant self-reliance.

Tragedy plunged us from the peak of success to the
depths of total dependence.

In the valley of shadows, we painfully learned to rely
on our Partner.

He comforted, healed.

Again, we drew in the sweet fragrance of our beloved
roses.

He lifted us to a higher pinnacle.

Not two alone, but with Him.

Again, we prosper,

For the love of God.

Jack Brothers

Carey marveled at the beauty of this simple story of faith. It raised her curiosity about Gavin and *his* faith.

"Dad and his brother rebuilt this business after a fire leveled it to the ground," Gavin explained, noting the questioning look in her eyes. "They were destitute at first, but the congregation from the local church gave them the help they needed to get started again. That was when the Jack brothers learned to rely on God."

"What about you, Gavin?" Carey looked him directly in the eye. "Do you have faith in God, or do you rely on yourself for success?"

Gavin looked away. Her pointed question had made him uncomfortable. "Carey, it's not that simple. The fire that happened nearly forty years ago was 'an act of God', the result of an electrical storm. It makes sense that 'God's people' would offer help. But I've had to deal with some pretty tough characters who would have destroyed me unless I fought back."

Gavin ran his hand through his hair. His own explanation seemed to make him uneasy. "Carey, this business has seen some prosperous times, and some difficult ones. As soon as you find success, there's someone out there waiting to steal it from you. I won't let that happen. When I see opportunities to do better for myself, I go after them. I don't expect God to condone my methods, but they work."

A sandy-haired youth entered the greenhouse. "Mr. Jack, excuse me. Could I speak with you?"

"Go on. I'll be fine," Carey insisted. She watched the spring-loaded door bang shut behind them. Memories of Gavin bringing her roses during her illness came to mind. He had told her then, "you have your faith, I have mine," and now she understood a little better what he'd meant.

Carey wandered toward the benches. She fingered a leaf hanging over the end of the rose bed. Immature plants filled the benches, showing barely developed, tight, green buds. She wondered what was keeping Gavin, and if it would be best to leave; yet no sooner had the thought crossed her mind when Gavin returned.

"There's not much to look at in this house. Follow me, and I'll show you some of the varieties in blossom." Gavin took long, powerful strides toward the opposite end of the greenhouse.

Carey, at five foot seven inches, usually found it necessary to shorten her stride when walking with others, but not with Gavin. She lengthened her stride to keep pace with him, and still he waited impatiently for her at the door to the next greenhouse.

With a minimum of explanation, Gavin pointed out the sweetheart varieties and full-size roses. He identified the commercial developer of the various strains

88

and watched Carey compare their unique fragrances.

When she'd seen every house, she hurried behind him down the long aisles returning toward the office, watching him swing his broad shoulders to avoid bumping the bench posts.

Just as she passed through the door in front of him, a low-slung red sportscar roared into the parking lot and screeched to a halt, blocking Carey's way to her van.

A strawberry-blonde woman alighted, designer-label, magenta coatdress flapping open in the breeze to reveal shapely, long legs. Her aristocratic, model-like features could have come directly off the most chic, high-fashion magazine cover.

"Gavin, I've been waiting ever so patiently at the house. I finally decided to come see for myself what could be keeping you." The obsequious woman wrapped long, manicured fingers about Gavin's arm, leaning into him.

Stunned and sickened, Carey felt her throat tighten with a suffocating sensation.

The woman leisurely released her grasp on Gavin's arm and turned to Carey. With the practiced eye of a soaring hawk, she scrutinized Carey. Seconds later, a look of haughty dismissal dominated her features.

"Gavin, your manners. Won't you introduce me to your friend?" she said in a silky, patronizing tone.

"Alissa, this is a customer of mine, Carey McIlwain. Carey, Alissa Redgrave." Gavin managed a perfunctory introduction in a reasonably normal tone, while his eyes avoided Carey's.

Carey swallowed past the golfball-sized lump lodged in her throat. "My pleasure," she forced the words out. Carey extended her hand, but Alissa ignored it. Awkwardly, Carey shoved it into her coat pocket.

"Now I'm certain you'll understand, Carey, if we excuse ourselves," Alissa continued in a throaty voice. "Gavin and I have personal matters to take care of, don't we, darling?" She squeezed Gavin's arm suggestively.

"Good day, Carey." Gavin's cool dismissal ripped fresh wounds inside Carey.

Gavin helped Alissa into her car, then settled in beside her. Alissa spun her tires, spitting gravel before turning up the drive to the sprawling white mansion. Carey realized Alissa's car was the one parked by the mansion when she had first arrived, and now she thought she understood the reason for Gavin's abrupt behavior.

Heavyhearted, Carey climbed into her truck. How could she have been such a fool, she asked herself. The indications that signaled Gavin's involvement with someone else had shouted at her, yet she had closed her eyes to them.

As her mind sorted through the reality of the situation, Carey admitted to herself with bitter disappointment that she and Gavin shared little in common. She had secretly harbored hopes that somehow the Lord would intervene, making her attraction to him justifiable, and Gavin's feelings for her as strong as hers for him.

With a female like Alissa by his side, alluring and provocative, the very antithesis of a God-fearing woman, the chances of that happening were all but nonexistent. Although Carey noted Gavin had not returned Alissa's gestures of affection, he could not remain unmoved by such an attractive and seductive woman.

Tears glistened on Carey's pale cheeks, and she choked back a sob as she turned the key in the ignition. In a short prayer to God, she asked for His comfort and guidance, and an especially large dose of grace to see her through future encounters with Gavin.

She pulled a tissue from her coat pocket. Floyd's map came with it. Carey dabbed away her tears and studied the route to Robinson's Supply. As she pulled away from Jack Brothers Roses, Carey never wanted to see the place again.

In the weeks following her acceptance of the harsh reality that Gavin could never be right for her, Carey viewed Alex with greater appreciation. At times, the possibility of her friendship with Alex turning into something more crossed her mind.

She tried to assess her feelings for him as she dressed to go to the college concert with him on Saturday night. She pulled on her wedgwood-blue dress made of the softest angora-blend yarn. It molded attractively to her feminine curves. The dress was Alex's favorite. He had told her so the first time he saw it, and now, she anticipated the appreciative and thoughtful comments it would bring.

Alex, always the gentleman, possessed a large store of appropriate compliments. She'd come to count on them, especially following the emotionally devastating encounter with Alissa. Compared with such a stunningly groomed beauty, Carey had taken inventory of herself and felt she was lacking. Thank goodness for Alex's vocal appreciation of her.

Carey brushed her auburn-brown hair vigorously and watched it settle, shining and vibrant, on her shoulders. The ends turned under with a gentle curl, exactly the way she'd planned when using her electric rollers.

With care, she applied her makeup. She didn't have flawless skin, so a good foundation was important. Carey's medium-peach complexion looked best with a peach-toned blusher. Small amounts of deep blue eye shadow enhanced the dark blue irises she had inherited from her mother. Dark brown mascara lengthened her lashes.

Standing back, she surveyed the overall effect. It pleased her. Carey snatched her evening bag from her dresser, rummaged through her purse for keys and a comb and tucked them inside. On her way to the closet, she grabbed a fistfull of tissues and stuffed them inside the black beaded bag.

Carey snapped on the light in the front closet. Shoving raincoats, overcoats, and ski parkas aside, she managed to locate her black dress boots, the ones with high heels and a calf-hugging shape, in the back corner.

She smiled to herself as she sat on the redwood boot box her father had crafted years ago, a box filled with ice skates in child's sizes from years gone by. Ordinarily, she would strap on her dressy, high-heeled shoes, but Alex's strenuous objections to her facing the winter cold in such flimsy footwear prevented her from even considering it. His protective attitude toward her since her bout with pneumonia bordered on excessive, but she considered it an admirable quality, nevertheless.

Carey straightened and pulled out her dressy black coat, then folded it carefully over the back of a dining chair. Alex would help her into it, perfectly mannered man that he was.

She answered the doorbell almost before it rang.

"Stand back and let me look at you," were his first words. "Outstanding." Alex's eyes moved appreciatively over her, from her hair to her toes, and back to settle on her pretty face.

Carey beamed, then came forward for a brief embrace. She felt the familiar security of his arms cradling her softly against him. "Thank you, kind sir," she whispered against his neck. She buried her face into his overcoat as she felt the pace of his breathing quicken.

After a few seconds, he leaned away from her. "Carey, I don't know what it is tonight, but I'm glad you're in such a funny, affectionate mood." He took her hand in his ample, strong one, then brought it up, brushing a gentle kiss across the back of it. Alex's warm, gold-green eyes glowed from within, while his expression stilled and grew serious. "We have a lot more to talk about. Later." Mock sternness wrinkled his forehead. "Now, come on. We'll miss the first movement."

"It's only Beethoven," she teased. "You're being unfair, keeping me in suspense like this. Tell me what it is you wanted to talk about."

"Carey, we'll have plenty of time later to talk," he murmured, his voice growing husky. "I intend to hear all of the Beethoven." Reluctantly, Alex stepped away from her.

"Alex, sometimes you're too much the gentleman," Carey grumbled affectionately, handing him her coat.

"If that's so, then put this on yourself, young lady." His hazel eyes sparkled as he teasingly returned her coat to the chair.

"Only kidding. I'd be devastated if you didn't hold my coat." Carey handed it back to him and slipped easily into it with his help.

They chatted freely about the events of the past week as Alex drove toward the college auditorium. He described the developments taking place in the college greenhouse, and Carey talked about the various customers who came into the shop, laughing over some of the strange requests, such as the woman who asked to have a plant she'd chosen from the front display case wired to Buffalo.

Carey walked down the auditorium aisle on Alex's arm, stepping neatly past the outside seats to a pair of vacant seats nearer the center, where past experience told her the acoustics would be much better.

Alex helped her remove her coat, positioning it comfortably over her shoulders. When he removed his own coat, Carey saw that he wore her favorite gray-tweed suit with a white shirt and striped gray tie. The combination lent him a dignified quality she admired.

They read their programs and chatted until the auditorium lights dimmed. When the symphony began the first movement of Beethoven's Ninth, Carey found herself increasingly curious, wondering what topic was so important that Alex wanted to keep it to himself until later.

Her curiosity increased as the second movement began, and she silently chided Beethoven for writing a fourth movement to his last symphony, even if it was the famous, "Ode to Joy." She determined to ply Alex with questions during the intermission before the third movement. What could cause his oddly serious-bordering-on-affectionate expression, one she'd never seen in the past?

Finally, the lights came up, and many in the audience moved to the lobby to stretch their legs. Carey looked down their row. A few people remained seated, but those on either side of them had vacated their places, leaving them a little privacy.

"I'm really on pins and needles, Alex," she half whispered. "What did you want to talk about?" A small, tentative smile curved her lips while her sapphire eyes plied his with curiosity.

Alex wrapped his fingers around hers. "This isn't the best time for my discussion." His voice was quietly tender, but insistent. "Let's wait until the concert is over." He placed her hand onto the armrest between them.

Carey forced her brows together and formed her

mouth into a little pout as she leaned her shoulder against his. "Alex Hensley, you're an unforgivable tease."

"Not nearly so unforgivable as you, my sweet," he bantered, his eyes widening in accusation.

Crimson stained her cheeks in spite of her efforts to suppress the blush. But she recovered quickly, letting out an audible sigh, intensifying the reaction with an exaggerated huff.

The lights dimmed again, and Carey resigned herself to sitting impatiently through the last two movements of the symphony before learning more.

As the music flowed around her, she pondered the possibility that Alex might be romantically much more serious about her than she was about him. Alex embodied many good qualities. He would do anything in the world for her. But was he someone with whom she wanted to be seriously involved?

That question bothered her, especially in light of her encounter with Gavin a few weeks earlier. Until then, she hadn't realized how Gavin could affect her. He could make her tremble without even the slightest touch and she could be devastated by his involvement with someone else. She wished she could forget that, but she couldn't.

At last, the concert ended. The final notes faded to enthusiastic applause by the audience. Alex helped Carey into her coat, then they slowly made their way to the back of the auditorium and into the chilling March air.

"My place?" Carey asked as Alex backed out of his parking spot.

"Only on one condition," he teased, resting his arm about her shoulders. "You have to promise to behave yourself."

"And if I don't?" Carey intertwined her fingers with his.

"That's simple. I'll never tell you what I was going to discuss with you tonight." In the dim light, Carey watched a mischievous expression turn the corner of his mouth upward.

At Carey's, Alex clicked on the stereo radio while she set a kettle of water on to boil. He was fiddling with the reception dial when she joined him in the living room.

Carey curled her stockinged feet beneath her legs and settled on the couch. Alex adjusted the radio volume and joined her there.

His golden green eyes searched hers, then his brow creased with concern. Suddenly, Carey wasn't sure she really wanted to know what Alex had on his mind.

"Something the matter, Carey? You look melancholy. Where did all that sparkle disappear to?"

Her face clouded with uneasiness. "I'm afraid I might have been unfair with you. Taken advantage."

"No. That's not true." His denial came without hesitation. Alex brought her hand to his lips and kissed her fingertips. "Teased, maybe, but never taken advantage of. Carey, I'm a grown man with my eyes wide open."

The tea kettle boiled, and Carey moved quickly to still its shrill whistle. She was thankful for the intrusion, sensing that the atmosphere had grown much too serious. A few minutes later, she returned with two cups of steaming chocolate and set them on the coffee table before joining Alex on the sofa again.

Alex ignored the refreshment and focused his attention squarely on her, a small furrow creasing his forehead. "Carey, I want you to come with me to Florida during spring break next month. Take some time off and tour the commercial growers." One corner of his mouth eased into a smile. "It would be a fantastic opportunity for us both, in more ways than one."

Carey fidgeted with the hem of her dress. "Alex, you can't be serious. Come with you on a trip?"

"I didn't mean it the way you think," he cut in. "I hope you know by now, I wouldn't dream of," he hesitated, "taking advantage of you."

Carey tossed her head back and laughed nervously. "Of course you wouldn't. You're the most honorable man I know."

"Then why did you react like that? It would give us an opportunity to get to know each other better, in a strictly wholesome sense, that is."

Carey shook her head. "Alex, I have a business to run. I can't leave that to someone else. We're approaching the busiest season, too. Easter. Mother's Day. Memorial Day." With her eyes, she implored him to understand. "As for getting to know one another better," her voice dropped, "maybe while you're in Florida, we can think about our relationship more objectively."

"I don't have to go to Florida alone to do that. I've done it right here in Stockport, all along." His voice grew insistent. "If I thought you'd accept, I'd—"

"Alex, don't." She cut him off quickly. "Can't we just go on as we have been?" Carey swallowed hard. How had she let the conversation lead to this? Unsettled, she moved across the room and stood in front of the television, her back to Alex. Her fingers idly stroked her father's bowling trophy. She felt Alex's eyes on her, knowing if she turned to look, she'd find that doleful quality she'd sometimes seen before. Carey heard him rise from the sofa and realized she couldn't let the evening end this way.

"Alex, don't go. Please." Carey went to him as he pulled on his coat. She touched his cheek, feeling the

97

bristle of his beard against her palm.

He pulled her hand away. "Carey, you're an enigma. When the evening started, you couldn't get enough of me, but as soon as I come your way, you back off. What is it you want from me, anyhow?" He finished buttoning his coat and picked up his gloves.

She hesitated, torn by conflicting emotions. She felt something special but undefinable for Alex. If she only knew exactly what that emotion was, she could end the discomfort for them both.

"I'm sorry. Truly, I am, but I guess I just can't answer you." Her words sounded pitifully inadequate.

Alex paused, his green gaze now boring into her.

"When you get it figured out, give me a call." His quiet statement contained no sarcasm. He left then, and Carey stood by the door, slightly stunned. She watched his car lights disappear down the street, then returned to the living room. Two stone-cold mugs of chocolate remained untouched on the coffee table. She carried them to the kitchen and emptied them in the sink with a murky splash.

Chapter Eight

Carey's business picked up throughout April and May, hitting a peak at Easter, and another at Mother's Day. But this time, instead of trying to work far more hours than usual during the rush periods, she called her cousins, Gail and Sue, for extra help.

Now with the Memorial Day chores also behind her, Carey found a few minutes to tidy up the greenhouse desk. It was so strewn with papers and second-class mail that she simply couldn't find anything on it. She sorted through stacks of magazines and newsletters. Rarely did she find time to read them. Catalogs, wire association publications, and old wire service directories as thick as telephone books thudded into the wastebasket.

She paused over a recent Flowers by Wire Association newsletter, one which went out regionally to the Rochester area association members. Its headline ran: "BIG BASH PLANNED FOR ANNUAL MEETING. City Center Hotel hosts dinner and lecture."

Carey knew the City Center Hotel's reputation—they catered the most extravagant events in the area. But reading further, she learned that her annual wire service dues included the dinner and lecture for herself and a guest.

She set the newsletter aside. Weeks had passed since her last date with Alex, the night he told her to call him when she figured out what she wanted. She hadn't called—yet. But she certainly had thought about it.

Could she tell him with a certainty that she knew now what she wanted from a relationship with him? No. But neither did she think she could find the answer unless she spent more time with him. The wire association event might provide just the opening she needed to put their relationship on a new footing.

Carey mulled over the situation as she sorted the rest of the paperwork. In the past several weeks, she had missed Alex's companionship, his tenderness. Certainly no one else had come along to take his place.

She had recovered completely from her ill-fated encounter with Gavin. Now, when he delivered her order each Wednesday morning, her pulse didn't even skitter. She only had to recall the image of him with Alissa to know that Gavin could have no special place in her heart.

Carey picked up the newsletter once again. It even carried a photo of the event held in the City Center Hotel last year. Many of the women wore long dresses. She tried to remember the last time she'd worn a long dress. Maybe it was when her friend, Julie, had gotten married. The attendant's gown hung in her closet waiting. She loved its pastel blue color and ruffly style, and she always felt very feminine when wearing it. The neck scooped ever so gently, framing her diamond pendant necklace against her throat.

Carey shook her head. If she wanted to see Alex, if she wanted to go to the City Center Hotel, she had to stop dreaming, pick up the phone, and dial his number.

"Maggie, it's stunning. You're so clever." Carey turned the white sweetheart rose corsage in her hand, then held it over her heart. The rosebuds, interspersed with baby's breath, rested against a background of blue lace. Several loops of a spaghetti-thin, pale-blue satin ribbon draped from the center of the corsage. "This is absolutely perfect. I love it." An approving look beamed from her face.

Maggie couldn't hide her satisfaction. "I'm glad you like it. Now go on and get yourself ready. I can close up tonight."

"I've got plenty of time," Carey insisted. "Alex isn't coming for another two hours."

Maggie turned Carey toward the side door and gave her a nudge. "Off with you. And have a wonderful time."

In a little less than two hours, Carey had showered, and washed and styled her hair. Wrapped in a summer-weight robe, she applied makeup in front of the bathroom mirror. She recalled the surprise in Alex's voice when she phoned to invite him out. It was exciting to be going to the formal dinner at the City Center Hotel.

Carey pulled her gown from the closet, untied the garment protector lacing at the top of the hanger, and slipped it from the clear plastic. She unzipped the dress and slid it over her head, feeling the satiny fabric slip over her, then settle on her shoulders. If the dress had any fault at all, it was that of making her appear younger than her twenty-four years.

White lace ruffles covered the entire skirt of the gown in narrow rows. Even the puffy short sleeves were ringed with the same delicate lace trim. Carey added the finishing touch—the diamond necklace her parents had given her when she graduated from college. It rested in the triangle at the base of her throat.

Carey fastened her white, thin-strapped sandals and brought the corsage from the refrigerator. She lifted it carefully from its nest of tissue and held it against the dress. Perfect. She admired it for a moment; then, hearing Alex's car in the driveway, Carey returned the corsage to its box, knowing Alex would want to pin it on her himself. She greeted him with a tentative smile.

"Carey, you're so lovely, it takes my breath away." His appreciative eyes stole over her.

"I've missed you, Alex." Her words carried a breathy quality she hadn't intended.

"And I, you." Pulling her closer with one hand around her shoulder, Alex kissed her hello. The soft pressure of his lips and the bristle of his mustache against her mouth caused a pleasant sensation.

When the kiss ended, he noticed the corsage and lifted it from the carton, pulling the corsage pin from the center. His fingers trembled slightly as he pinned the roses on Carey's shoulder. Alex's neck reddened as his fingers touched her bare skin. When he finished, he stood back to admire the effect.

"The perfect finishing touch." He placed her hand in the crook of his arm. "Shall we go?"

During the forty-five minute drive to Rochester, Alex told Carey about his trip to Florida. He described the thousand and one various exotic plants, giving particularly long descriptions of the Heliconia varieties.

Carey shared the successful story of her busy holiday season, explaining that her cousins had helped out.

"You mean Todd didn't come home to help?" Alex voiced dismay. "I certainly hope he'll be in Stockport to work during the summer. You've shouldered the responsibility for that business alone long enough."

"He'll be in summer school, Alex. He takes the last classes toward his Master's degree then. I don't under-

102

stand your concern. I've done all right without him," Carey defended.

"Of course you have. I didn't mean to imply otherwise. It just seems unfair, that's all." Alex patted her hand.

"I learned life isn't always fair last October. Now, do you think we could talk about something else? How are Scotty and Jody? I haven't seen them in ages."

Conversation for the remainder of the trip noticeably lacked controversy, so by the time Alex drove into the City Center Hotel parking ramp, they were totally at ease with one another again.

The decor of the grand, old refurbished hotel never failed to fascinate Carey. The first thing she noticed as they entered was the gigantic chandelier hanging in the center of the lobby. Though she'd seen it before, she stood admiring its sparkling beauty while Alex asked at the desk for the exact directions to the banquet room. Then, with his hand on Carey's back, he guided her down the carpeted hallway toward a large room already buzzing with conversation.

Carey entered the red carpeted room on Alex's arm, her eyes sweeping the formally dressed crowd. Her eyes immediately lighted on Alissa Redgrave's stunning figure standing beside the darkly handsome Gavin Jack. They stood talking with an older man, one on whom Alissa frequently leaned during her conversation.

Somewhat shaken, Carey tried to imagine why Gavin would attend such an event. He didn't retail any flowers, so he wouldn't be a member of the wire association. Yet, here he was, smartly attired in a dark blue suit tailored to make the most of his powerful physique, with an aristocratic and dazzling female who made Carey feel like an unsophisticated schoolgirl.

Alissa spotted Carey and Alex, and Carey felt her inner reserves evaporate when Alissa clutched Gavin's arm and started toward them.

"Alex, do you think we could…" Carey stammered nervously.

"Carey, what is it? You're white as a sheet?" Alex asked in surprise. "Maybe you need some fresh air."

Carey desperately tried to think of a way to avoid the encounter, but outmaneuvering Alissa proved impossible.

"I'll be fine," she choked, swallowing the despair in her throat as the stunning Alissa homed in on them. Carey gave a forced smile and a tense nod.

"Carey McIlwain, isn't it?" Alissa quickly assessed Carey with gray eyes as hard as glacial ice. "Won't you introduce your friend?" The sleek woman appeared taller and more striking than Carey recalled. She wore a long, clingy, black gown, slit from ankle to knee and cut low at the neck to reveal creamy flesh.

"Alissa, Dr. Hensley." Carey made the briefest of introductions.

Carey noticed Alissa's quick reappraisal upon hearing the title "Doctor."

"Hello, Doctor." Alissa purred, her expression warming with interest. "Gavin, honey, meet Dr. Hensley."

Gavin shifted his weight uneasily. Carey noticed that he carefully avoided making eye contact with her. "Alex and I have met." Gavin nodded with a jerk. Alex wordlessly complied.

"Gavin, see that Carey and Alex are seated with us, will you, darling? I'll go rescue Daddy from his circle of admirers." Alissa glided skillfully between conversation groups. Carey noticed how easily she charmed those around her father, linking her arm in his and extracting him from their midst.

Gavin, his expression distant and unreadable,

showed Carey and Alex to the long table at the front of the banquet hall.

"This can't be right," Carey protested, scanning the place cards at the head table. "We don't belong here. This is for honored guests." Her complexion colored.

"Don't be silly," Alissa responded, joining them before Carey and Alex could escape to a different table. "There's plenty of room here, and I insist you join us." Alissa quickly moved place settings apart, calling to a uniformed waiter.

Carey's embarrassment escalated when an argument between the headstrong Alissa and an equally adamant waiter ensued. Carey turned her back to the scene wishing to ignore it, while Mr. Redgrave watched his daughter in action with a knowing grin.

"That's my Alissa. Inherited her willfulness from me, I admit." Mr. Redgrave shifted focus to Carey. "Did I understand that you're Carey McIlwain, daughter of Patrick and Helen McIlwain, of Stockport? I'm Winston Redgrave, Redgrave Greenhouses." His hand shot out.

Suddenly, Carey understood. Winston Redgrave owned the largest florist operation in Monroe County. He grew most of his own cut flowers and potted plants, which supplied his ever-expanding chain of retail outlets.

"Now, Dr. Hensley, you can seat your companion. Everything's arranged." Alissa slipped her arm through Alex's to show him the exact place. Alex held Carey's chair, then squeezed into his seat between her and Alissa. The two added place settings cramped the already crowded head banquet table, and Carey resented Alissa's strategically placing herself between Gavin and Alex, but she remained silent. Winston Redgrave took his place to Carey's left.

Waiters served the appetizers—shrimp-stuffed celery,

marinated cocktail mushrooms, and salmon-stuffed egg. In spite of their appealing appearance, Carey found she had lost her appetite. She nibbled a mushroom at Winston's urging.

"Carey, you're very quiet down there," Alissa complained. "Maybe you could pick up some pointers from Daddy and get your business back in shape."

Carey tried hard to think of an appropriate response as the bite of marinated mushroom turned sour in her mouth, but the only retort that came to mind was too sharp to use.

Gavin seemed uneasy and a bit sullen, and Carey could only assume it had to do with her and Alex's presence at the event. She knew Gavin held no great regard for Alex.

"Dr. Hensley, tell me about yourself." Alissa coyly trained her attention on the man at her left.

Obviously flattered by Alissa's interest, Alex shifted slightly in his chair, to an angle favoring her. "I teach botany at Stockport College. I'm in charge of the college greenhouse, and my specialty is exotic plants. I'm personally interested in Heliconias."

"How absolutely fascinating, Alex," Alissa drawled in contrived interest. "I bet you know more about Heliconias than anyone else in this room." Alissa leaned in Alex's direction, placing her left hand on his forearm in a proprietary manner.

Carey's eyes riveted on Alissa's left fourth finger. A large diamond engagement ring sparkled back at her.

How could Gavin tolerate such brash flirtations from his fiancée? Why was Alex responding to Alissa's false behavior? Alissa was no more interested in Alex than she was in jumping off a bridge into the Erie Canal. Alissa had one mission tonight—to make Carey McIlwain suffer constant waves of humiliation and embarrassment. And she was off to a remarkably successful start.

At the end of the table Winston Redgrave appeared oblivious to his daughter's transparent behavior, occasionally commenting to Carey about the delicious food being served. Nevertheless, Carey was grateful to share the small talk with him, since Alex was monopolized by Alissa.

When Carey finished her meal, she excused herself from the table, saying she wished to freshen up before the speaker began. Her explanation was only partially true. She desperately needed breathing space between herself and Alissa before she lost control of her tongue and said something she'd regret.

No sooner had Carey reached the hallway outside the banquet room, than a grip on her upper arm halted her. She turned and stared into Gavin's smouldering black eyes, his broad shoulders set in a rigid stance.

"What's the matter with you? Are you trying for the martyr-of-the-year award? Why didn't you tell Alissa off? She walked all over you, and you sat there and quietly accepted her trampling."

Stunned at Gavin's outpouring, Carey stared at his tense, brooding features. "Gavin Jack, I don't understand how you can talk about your own fiancée that way. Doesn't the woman you love deserve more loyalty?"

Gavin released her arm. "Where Alissa's concerned, it's not a question of love. It's strictly business. When I marry her, my business merges with Redgrave's." His cold words made Carey shiver.

"Aren't you paying too big a price for whatever benefits a Redgrave merger could offer? Think about it, Gavin, and about your future happiness," she urged.

"Carey, you don't know the half of it. Redgrave has

paved the way for me, groomed me to be his right-hand man. He arranged it so I could give a speech tonight, a speech that will give me the credibility necessary to become the top rose supplier in the area. My future success and Redgrave's are tied together. Alissa is just part of the package deal."

Carey stared at Gavin, taking in what he had said. After a few moments, the pieces fell into place. "I'd noticed a change in your appearance months ago, and the fact that you had become so aloof. Now I understand why. You were making your Redgrave connection." Sadness and pity welled up in her, filling her eyes with moisture. "Please excuse me," she murmured, moving past Gavin toward the restroom.

Struggling to hold back more tears, Carey dabbed a tissue at the corners of her eyes and stared at her reflection. She was determined to control her emotions and hear Gavin's speech. Composed, she returned to the banquet hall and slipped quickly into her seat.

Gavin gave an articulate speech, informative and authoritative. Geared to the rose market, he outlined several methods of increasing rose sales and improving deliveries.

Alex reached for Carey's hand, startling her from her world of private thoughts. They exchanged glances, and Carey knew from the look on his face, Alex had been staring at her. She wondered for how long, and whether her innermost thoughts had registered unconsciously across her face.

Carey caught a glimpse of Alissa's expression. A sort of smug, gloating look spread across her face as she leaned back and listened to Gavin's words. Suddenly she drew a small pad and pen from her purse and scribbled a note. Then she leaned across Alex to hand it to Carey. Before realizing the note was meant for Winston,

Carey's eyes had absorbed the words: "Gavin's image is just right tonight, don't you agree, Dad?" Thoroughly embarrassed, Carey quickly passed the note on to Redgrave.

He read the note and tipped his head to Alissa, self-satisfaction clearly showing on his face.

As the audience applauded Gavin, Carey inconspicuously rose from her place, indicating to Alex she wished to leave. At least she could spare herself further unpleasantness by removing herself from Alissa's company.

In the parking lot Alex opened the passenger's door and helped Carey in. The drive home began in a long silence, eventually broken by Alex.

"That was a different Gavin than I remember meeting last fall. He's really smoothed out the rough edges. Don't you think?"

"I guess so," Carey idly answered, still lost in her own thoughts.

They said little more until Alex pulled into Carey's driveway. When the car stopped Alex reached for Carey, tipped her chin up and searched her face, inquiry in his hazel eyes. He lowered his mouth to kiss her, and she closed her eyes in anticipation. But the picture of Gavin standing at the speaker's podium sprang into her mind. Her eyes flew open, and she broke forcefully from Alex.

"Alex, I'm sorry. I didn't mean…" desperately, Carey searched for the right words.

Alex stared at her, his expression like someone who had been struck in the face.

"I think I'd better go in now," she offered lamely. "You understand, don't you?" Carey reached for the doorhandle.

Alex barred her escape. "No, Carey. I don't understand. I thought you'd finally straightened your thinking out when you called me this week, but suddenly we're right back where we started."

Alex gave her a questioning look mingled with remorse. "Carey, listen to me," he pleaded. "We're right for each other. We're both people of strong faith, and I love you very much. I'd care for you every minute of every day, if you'd let me. I can't go on waiting patiently in the wings for you to decide what course your heart wants to take."

Tormented by confusing emotions, Carey looked away. She focused her eyes on the porch lamp, not trusting herself to speak. Never had she expected such intense feelings from Alex, and she wondered if he surmised her feelings for Gavin. She swallowed to suppress the stubborn lump in her throat.

"I didn't mean for things to turn out this way, Alex. I'm sorry. Please believe me." She reached for the doorhandle again. This time he didn't stop her.

Carey let herself out. Alex roared out of the driveway and down the street. As she turned the key and stepped inside, Carey asked herself a thousand questions all at once.

Chapter Nine

"Hi, Sis!"

"Todd! What are you doing here?" Carey shut off the water and shoved her hose beneath the bench of poinsettia cuttings she'd been watering.

Todd dropped from the shop into the first greenhouse, taking the two steps down with one stride of his long legs.

"Sis, you look great. This business must agree with you." He planted a brotherly kiss on her cheek. Carey immediately noticed the marked change in his attitude toward her since New Year's. He stepped back and looked her over closely. "Except you look tired. How about some assistance? You must be working too hard." Concern brought his brows together.

"Todd, you're kidding. Aren't you? I thought summer school ended *next* month, not in the middle of July." Carey followed Todd as he wandered between the benches, compulsively inspecting the poinsettia cuttings Floyd had taken last week. Todd paused, fingering the leaf of one of the cuttings.

"Sis, it's a good thing I came. Look at this." Carey bent over the leaf Todd indicated.

At first, the leaf looked like all the others to Carey.

111

Then, taking a closer look, she saw what Todd meant. The edges of the leaf seemed to be rotting.

"*Botrytis cinerea*. Gray mold. You need to keep the air at night circulating to decrease the humidity." Todd's confident diagnosis carried the weight of several years' schooling at the agricultural college at Cornell. He leaned against the bench, tapping his fingertips together anxiously, and cocked one eyebrow at Carey.

"What should I do?" Carey's stomach turned sour. Now, several months after her parents' deaths, she had just managed to work the business's balance sheets into the black by a reasonable margin. She couldn't bear to think what would happen if the poinsettia crop failed.

"Sis, don't waste a minute worrying about it. I'll take care of everything." Todd picked up several of the infected cuttings.

"But Todd..."

"Trust me. It's almost closing time, isn't it? I'm ready for one of your great home-cooked suppers. Why don't you go count the cash in the drawer so we're ready to leave the minute the clock strikes five." Todd disappeared down the aisle into the potting room in the back.

Still puzzled, Carey prepared the shop for closing. She intuitively sensed a restlessnes about Todd and wondered what he really had on his mind.

"What's Todd after? More money?" Maggie asked suspiciously.

"He says he wants to work here—that I need his help." Carey stuffed the bills from the cash register tray into a bank pouch. "And he's already diagnosed a problem with the poinsettia cuttings, and it could worsen if it isn't taken care of immediately." Carey adjusted the cash register for the next day's business.

"Seems a shame to accuse him of it before he asks,

but I've never seen your brother lift a finger without some ulterior motive," Maggie warned. "And money always figures in it somewhere."

"I hear you," Carey responded flatly, casting a glance of suspicion in Maggie's direction.

Carey tore off the register tape totals and shoved the readout into the money pouch with the bills. She zipped the pouch and tossed it into the safe, then spun the dial.

Maggie swept the last of the scraps from the floor beneath the arranging table and dumped them into the trash. Floyd and Todd, immersed in conversation, came in from the back.

"Time to call it quits. You fellows can catch up tomorrow," Carey said, turning the night latch on the side door.

Maggie and Floyd said good night. Todd waited for Carey, then closed the door behind her and checked the lock. He fell into step beside his sister as they walked the short distance home.

"You haven't done too badly for a teacher, Carey. Of course, with my added expertise, the business will soon be blooming and booming." Todd's chatter had more than a hint of nervousness.

"There's one quality that has always amazed me about you, Todd," Carey said, unlocking the door to the house.

"What's that, Sis? My astounding intellect?" Todd picked the evening paper up from the doorstep.

"Your total lack of modesty," she answered dryly.

Todd threw back his head, but his laugh was tight and nervous.

Carey waited for Todd to plop into the easy chair, then sat rigidly on the edge of the sofa. Todd hid behind the front page of the evening paper.

"O.K., Todd. Out with it. What are you doing here?"

He lowered the paper halfway. "What are you talking about?" His question mocked innocence. "I'm here to take up my share of responsibility for the family business. That's all." The corner of his mouth twitched into a half-smile.

"In the middle of the last term for your Master's degree? No way, Brother. What happened?" Carey persisted. "Did you flunk out?"

Irritated, Todd brought the newspaper to his lap with a loud rumple. "No. I did not flunk out. If you must know, Amy and I broke up, and I'm depressed about it, so I decided to take some time off."

"I'm sorry," Carey apologized. "Do you want to talk about it?" she quietly asked, thinking Todd's first experience with rejection must be particularly painful. He'd always called the shots with women, as long as Carey could remember.

Worry lines creased his forehead. "No, I don't," he replied calmly, "but I'm really starved. I'd appreciate it if we could have dinner soon." He smiled his impish smile which had charmed others into action ever since he was a small boy.

Carey grinned, then went to Todd and kissed his cheek. "Welcome home, Brother. Dinner will be on in half an hour."

Relieved that Todd hadn't come to Stockport for money after all, Carey hummed to herself as she worked in the kitchen.

Forty-five minutes later, the last of the meat loaf she had made disappeared into Todd's mouth.

"Sis, you've learned a lot since the last time I ate here. This was fantastic." Todd gulped his remaining iced tea. Carey waited for him to counter the compliment by finding fault somewhere else, as he usually did. Expec-

114

tation must have shown on her face.

"What's the matter. Don't you believe me?" he asked innocently.

"Let's just say I've never known you to dish out a compliment without a complaint." Carey watched his expression carefully. Todd appeared falsely complacent.

"Since you brought it up, I do have one little complaint with life. Nothing to do with you. Just a sticky little problem some cash could solve." Todd nervously worked his napkin into a compact little ball and tossed it on his plate. His deep blue eyes searched Carey's. "Can you help me get fifteen grand?"

"Fifteen what?" Carey's words lacked volume. She stared in shock and disbelief, her head moving slowly from side to side. "Surely you don't mean what I think you just said."

"I need fifteen thousand to pay off a loan shark." Todd spoke desperately.

The meaning of his somber words bored into her. "Why did you borrow fifteen thousand dollars from a loan shark?" She struggled to control her inner turmoil.

"To pay off my debts." Todd parceled out the answer.

"What debts, Todd? Stop stringing me along like this and tell me the whole story!" Her stomach knotted as her mind spun with confusion.

"I've just hit a bad streak. That's all. I need the money to tide me over until I start winning again. You'll get it all back. The horses are running again next weekend. I'll make good. Until then, I've got to lie low, unless I want to get hurt—bad." Todd searched her eyes for understanding.

Carey paced across the room, nearly suffocating under the weight of Todd's problem. She inhaled deeply. Todd needed her, perhaps now more than ever before. No matter what he had done, she would stick by him as

115

long as she could help. But he needed more than her help. Todd needed professional counseling for his problem. Her mind raced, searching for feasible answers. She pressed her cold, clammy hands to her cheeks on this hot July evening. With concentrated effort, she regained control of her nerves. She prayed for the strength to do what had to be done—to help Todd repay his debts and to overcome his gambling problem. She returned to her place across from Todd at the table with a new conviction.

"I'll loan you the money, little brother, but only on the condition that you get counseling. There are help groups dealing with this sort of illness."

"Illness?" Todd interrupted sharply. "I'm not sick, I'm just overextended," he defended hotly.

"I'm not going to argue semantics with you, Todd. If you have debts totaling fifteen thousand, you have a problem. The first step toward recovery is admitting you have a problem. Now, do you want my help or not?"

Todd chewed on his lower lip. He searched for some chink in her armored proposal, but found none. "O.K. I'll get help. When can you get me the money?"

"I'll apply for a loan tomorrow. It's the best I can do. The rest is up to the bank." Carey paused, hoping Todd would express some gratitude, but he left the table in brooding silence. She cleared away the dishes and washed them in solitude.

The month of July was a lovely one in Stockport. Hot sunny weather bolstered Carey's spirits. In spite of her personal problems early in the month, the brilliant days sped by, and Carey noted with regret that August was only a week off.

Todd proved himself a conscientious worker at any

116

task Carey assigned, whether helping Floyd take poinsettia cuttings or assisting Maggie with the retailing. And his charm added to the congenial air in the shop.

The bank had honored her request for an emergency loan. Todd gladly cosigned. The loan officer made it clear that he would only grant the request if they put up the florist business as collateral. Their parents had left the business to Carey and Todd mortgage-free. Only suppliers had clamored for payments in the early days following the funeral.

Payments to the bank each month would eat into the slim margin of savings Carey had slowly built up over the past several months. But she believed that, with God's guidance, she could keep up financially and help Todd overcome the problem that had brought on the unwanted debt.

The loan secured, Todd kept his promise to attend sessions of the Gamblers Anonymous Association. He drove to Rochester for the weekly meetings, but spoke little about what he did there. Although curious, Carey refrained from asking about the meetings. *No need making Todd's battle more difficult,* she told herself.

In spite of the disastrous circumstances that had brought him into the family business earlier than expected, Todd's added help at the greenhouse yielded some advantages. It allowed Carey to spend more time on music. While engrossed in the challenges of teaching budding guitarists, Carey completely escaped the stress of business and family problems. In fact, it was the only time she could forget them.

Along with Sarah, Billy, and Jason, who had taken guitar lessons from Carey since early January, two more young students, a brother and sister, had asked for lessons during the summer. Carey now took Wednesday mornings off to schedule each of them for a half hour of private instruction in her home.

Often, Carey stepped outside between lessons to take a breather or speak to one of the mothers doing the chauffering while the next child got out his instrument and warmed up. From her front porch, Carey could easily observe the comings and goings of customers at the shop three buildings away.

Like clockwork, Gavin Jack pulled up on this last Wednesday in July to make his regular rose delivery. She avoided even brief contacts with Gavin by scheduling lessons as she had, and was thankful for a reason not to see him.

Perhaps Alex had been more correct in his assessment of her feelings than she had been willing to admit nearly a month ago after their evening at the wire association dinner. She really didn't know what course her heart should take.

Carey stepped inside and took up her guitar. Sarah Campbell had warmed up long enough.

"Sarah, what am I going to do with you? You've almost finished another book." Carey winked at her student. Sarah had played her lesson well as usual.

Sarah beamed. "I like practicing the duets. Can we get another book of duets?"

"I'll see what I can find. Now, remember to work on the scales this week. They're just as important as playing duets."

Sarah wrinkled her freckled nose. Carey grinned, then wrote next week's date above the new assignments in Sarah's book. As usual, the lesson ended before they had accomplished everything Carey had intended.

Carey walked out onto the front porch with Sarah and waved to Mrs. Campbell who waited in the car for her daughter. Usually Billy Reed waited anxiously for his turn. Carey looked down the street toward the florist shop for the familiar yellow VW his mother drove.

Her attention riveted on Todd and Gavin. They stood talking next to Gavin's van. Carey wondered what topic they could be discussing so seriously, for she didn't think the two had ever exchanged more than perfunctory greetings.

Billy's mother pulled into the driveway. Carey's thoughts returned to her student and how she could entice him into practicing with the same regularity that he played little league baseball.

"Maggie, don't worry about a thing. I can handle it," Carey insisted, pushing the Emerys out the door two hours before closing time the following Friday afternoon.

"I feel guilty leaving you with such a pile of work," Maggie lamented. "What a shame the burden for this big wedding fell on you."

"When is there a summer weekend without a wedding? It comes with the territory." Carey picked up Maggie's handbag and slipped it over the woman's arm. "You and Floyd just concentrate on having a wonderful trip. Now, you'd better get out of here before the traffic gets any worse. And send us a card!" Carey waved as the couple backed out of the greenhouse driveway.

Scanning the remaining orders for the wedding tomorrow, Carey realized she'd have to stay after hours and work late into the night. Once again the responsibilities of the business crowded in on her. How unlike the feeling she had during the Wednesday morning guitar sessions.

Fortunately, Todd had picked up enough expertise in floral designing to help wire and tape the cut flowers for her. Together, maybe they could knock out the orders by ten o'clock that night. But until closing time,

Todd had his hands full taking over for Floyd in the back.

Carey brought a dozen roses from the cooler and began designing the maid-of-honor's bouquet. Gradually, she finished the bouquets and boutonnieres for the wedding party. Her next task involved arranging mums, roses, and carnations into centerpieces for the reception hall. She had just stepped into the cooler when she heard Todd call her name.

"Carey, let's go." His voice filtered past the partially opened cooler door. "Did you close out the cash register yet?"

She glanced at her watch. Only five minutes till closing. "Not yet, Todd. Could you do it while I clean up here?" Carey shut the heavy cooler door behind her.

"Sure. But make it snappy." Hot and tired, Todd combed his fingers through his reddish-brown hair, then moved his broad shoulders up and down to loosen tight muscles. "I'm going out tonight, and I know how long it takes you to get dinner on the table." He moved with long purposeful strides to the cash register, turned the key, and punched the various buttons.

Carey bit her tongue. In spite of Todd's attractive qualities, his personality often failed to charm her. "I need your help here tonight, Todd. Can't you arrange your date for another time?"

Todd shook his head while counting the bills. Carey waited to speak until he'd finished.

"But you knew about the wedding and the Emerys going on vacation. I've got several hours of work left here, even *with* your help." Her anxiety was clear in her words.

Todd scowled into the safe, his brows knitting together as he shoved documents aside to make room for the pouch. "I didn't know about any of that when I made this date."

"Well, break it," Carey said, irritated. She stooped to fill the dustpan.

Aware of her annoyance, he tried to coax her into a better mood. "Come on, Sis. Lighten up." A boyish smile crept over his features. He took the broom and dustpan from her and slipped his arm around her waist. "You handle this one alone tonight, and I'll make it up to you. I'll even set everything up for the wedding tomorrow, and you won't have to lift a finger."

"I won't have a finger left to lift. They'll be worked to the nubs while you're out on the town." In spite of herself she smiled as she took back the broom and dustpan and leaned them in the corner.

Todd never mentioned where he planned to go, and Carey didn't ask. Except for his Gamblers Anonymous meetings, he hadn't gone out since his return to Stockport.

Todd showered and left the house immediately after dinner. His parting words to his sister were "Don't wait up." Carey, realizing she'd be coming home late to an empty house, turned on the porch light and left the light on near the dining table inside.

Alone with her work and her thoughts, Carey listened to the quiet strains of FM radio. This wedding would be a particularly large one. With love songs floating in the background, she began to ponder what her own wedding might be like some day.

Certainly flowers would be the least of her worries. She favored roses, white ones for her bouquet, and yellow for her attendants, almost the same as the bride had requested for tomorrow.

A good photographer wouldn't be hard to find. Jim Glessing had always taken her family's photos, and he had such a way with people, they looked totally natural.

Her dress, white lace on satin, would have one of those high Victorian necks. Slim long sleeves would taper to her wrists, and the gathered skirt would fall to the floor in graceful folds from her hips.

Suddenly, Carey realized the major ingredient lacking from her fantasy was a suitable bridegroom. Yet she refused to be depressed over it. She was turning to the Lord more often in recent months, and she trusted that when the time was right, marriage would be a part of His plan for her.

The waiting didn't get any easier for her, though. With Alex, upstanding Christian that he was, she had thought she might be on the right track.

Gavin's tall, lean form sprang unbidden to mind. Certainly the Lord didn't intend her to interpret the strange interweaving of her path with Gavin's as a result of any guidance from Him.

The hour grew late. The hands on the clock neared midnight when Carey twisted wire around the center of the last bow to be used as a pew marker.

She cleaned up the arranging table and floor, flicked off all but the display window lights, then slung her bag over her shoulder and locked the door behind her. The still evening air felt hot and muggy as she moved down the driveway and turned toward home.

As she reached the top step of the porch, Carey heard the loud downshifting of a sports car motor. The sports car accelerated, then screeched to a halt in her driveway, its headlights blinding her. She jammed her key at the door lock.

Chapter Ten

"Carey!" With her heart in her throat, Carey turned and faced the sports car driver.

"Gavin, what are you doing here?" His form hulked over her in the dim porch light.

"Burning the midnight oil so little brother Todd can have the night out? Isn't that just like a devoted big sister?" Gavin's words were sharp and scornful.

"It's really none of your business, Gavin."

"Maybe not, but it certainly is *yours*. Your little brother sold you down the river in a poker game tonight, Carey. I tried to prevent it, but Todd wouldn't listen."

Gavin's words stung her. She quickly dismissed his accusation. Todd went to group sessions. He went to work. Until tonight he hadn't dated. Surely he had control of his gambling. He'd told her so himself.

"Why don't you go home to Alissa?" she cried defensively. "She's practically your wife, isn't she? What would she say if she knew you were with another woman?"

"*With another woman*?" he snapped. Even in the dim light, Carey could see the sudden change on his face. He moved closer and tenderly lifted her face in one hand. "That's quite an exaggeration on your part, Carey, but I might as well let you believe what you want to believe."

Gavin turned and quickly left. His tires squealed as the car accelerated. Carey watched the taillights disappear in the darkness, then let herself into the house alone—and lonely. She knew deep inside she cared for this strange, changeable man.

The next morning, Carey knocked on Todd's bedroom door. She didn't remember hearing him come in last night. When he didn't respond, she opened it a crack. His bed was empty.

Sleepy-eyed, Carey readied herself for work. Then she remembered—someone had to deliver the flowers for the big wedding. Without Todd, that someone was her. She slammed her fist against the kitchen table.

"Todd, why do you do this to me?" Tears of frustration burned in her eyes. "Can't you grow up and accept responsibility like an adult?"

Carey called her cousin Gail and asked her to watch the shop while she delivered the wedding order. By midmorning, Carey had made the trip to the church, carted in all the boxes and arrangements, and returned to the shop. Todd still had not come to work.

Worried, Carey phoned some of Todd's old high-school friends, but none had been with him the previous night nor seen him that morning.

Gavin was the only person Carey could think of who might know where Todd was, but she'd never call him. He'd lied to her last night about Todd's gambling. What further lies would he tell her today?

Still, as Carey watered the hanging plants in the greenhouse, she found herself doubting her brother. Suppose Gavin was right, and Todd had been gambling last night? What if he had gotten involved in other kinds of gambling? Wouldn't that explain his failure to show up for work this morning?

Just when it seemed that calling the police was her only alternative, Todd lumbered down the greenhouse aisle toward Carey.

"I'll do that, Sis," he offered, his voice listless and quiet. He took the hose from her and turned away.

"Todd, where have you been? I've been worried sick over you."

"Just out, that's all."

"Out where? Gambling?" The question came against her will.

"Of course not," he denied quickly. "Now, why don't you send Gail home and take care of the shop? I don't need you back here in my way all afternoon."

Too angry to speak, Carey turned to leave.

"And Sis?"

"What?" she barked, swinging around to face him again.

"Sorry I didn't deliver the wedding order this morning. Did everything go O.K.?" Todd apologized meaningfully.

"Just fine," she answered, puzzled over the tenderness showing through.

As the day wore on, Carey wondered more and more what, if not gambling, had kept Todd away so long. Gavin obviously knew something, but she wouldn't call him. Her mind still spun in confusion over their strange encounter the night before.

In fact, throughout the afternoon hours, her thoughts played over and over again the scene on her porch— Gavin's voice, with its power to evoke such strong responses in her. Her reaction to him scared her.

Many questions plagued her as she prepared to close the shop for the weekend.

She and Todd walked home in silence. One look told Carey he was deep in thought. He unlocked the door and held it for her. She couldn't remember ever seeing Todd so worried. He slumped into the easy chair without a word.

"I'll rustle up some hamburgers in a few minutes," she offered, remembering the scene of the evening before.

"Take your time, Sis. I haven't got any plans." Todd's blue eyes met hers for the first time that day. "Carey, I'm really sorry I messed up. I didn't mean to."

Carey searched his eyes. "Sure, little brother." She patted his arm, then turned away. She couldn't bring herself to press Todd about the preceding night.

Soon after dinner, Carey fell asleep, exhausted from working late the previous night and her worry over Todd that morning. Sunday morning dawned bright and warm, and Carey rose early and prepared waffle batter. She would bake several before church, eat what she wanted, and leave the rest for Todd, who was not an early riser.

Much to her surprise, Todd rose and showered in time to join her at the kitchen breakfast table. The worry lines in his brow stared back at her from across the table.

"I think we need to talk, Sis," Todd said, refusing her offer of a waffle fresh from the iron.

"Go ahead, little brother. I know something terribly important is on your mind." She touched her finger to his forehead. "You've done nothing but put wrinkles there since yesterday afternoon."

Todd's boyish expression turned even more vulnerable. "Don't make it harder on me by saying you understand. I don't deserve your understanding for what I've done."

"You'd better tell me what it is, then." Carey's mouth twitched into a nervous grin. "I suspect you got into a little poker game night before last."

Todd shook his head slowly from side to side. "How I wish now that were true—that it was just a simple penny ante poker game."

"Did you lose a lot?" she asked, wondering how she could possibly borrow again with the payments against the fifteen thousand dollar loan already gobbling up all her excess cash.

"I lost half the business." Anguish clouded Todd's eyes.

Carey gulped convulsively, "How could you do that!" She shuddered with a chill in spite of the hot humid weather.

"I didn't mean to, but I wound up in a real heavy game. Redgrave backed me. Said he'd make good on my debts. When all was said and done, he owned my half of McIlwain Greenhouses."

Carey's face paled. She stood and paced across the kitchen. From the window, she could see the florist shop and the patch of driveway next to its side door. Her thoughts reeled.

"Gavin Jack. He figures into this somewhere, doesn't he? Did he connect you with Redgrave?" Her words spewed out faster as she recalled Todd and Gavin in a long conversation that Wednesday morning.

"No," Todd responded flatly.

"Don't lie to me again, Todd. You've done enough of that already. Gavin connected you two, didn't he?" she hotly insisted.

"It's not like you think. I asked Gavin about Redgrave, that's all," Todd countered.

"That's all?" she asked, incredulous. "That's all he needed. Once Gavin knew you were ripe for the picking, he brought in Winston for the kill. I should have known. He's merging his growing business to Redgrave Greenhouses. This will just add to the pot." Carey paced nervously, her stomach tied in knots.

"Believe what you want, Carey. You always do anyway. I've never seen anyone so sure of the facts, the *wrong* facts." Todd rose. "When you get back from church, I'll be gone."

"Todd, wait. Where are you going?" Carey begged. "We can fight this thing, if only you'll try. Running away won't solve anything."

"I did try." Todd moved his head from side to side. "Leaving will solve one problem. I won't be around to make life more miserable for you than it already is. I want to get away from Stockport and everything that reminds me of failure." Todd stormed out, letting the screen door slam behind him.

Carey listened as Todd drove away. How could she face Gavin as a business partner? That's what it would come down to, even though Todd said it was Redgrave's money. Her mind whirled erratically. She'd go to Gavin. She'd offer to buy Todd's share of the business. Maybe he'd be able to persuade Redgrave to go along with it. Moments later, Carey was driving toward Medeena, fighting the impulse to push the gas pedal all the way to the floor.

She formulated her speech as she went. Gavin would receive a double dose from her—one for his collusion with Todd and the other for thinking he could own her family's business.

Half an hour later, Carey pulled up in front of Jack Brothers Roses, next to Gavin's delivery van. She glanced toward the mansion. No red sports car stood in the circular drive.

The door to the business opened easily. Carey called

Gavin's name. When he didn't answer, she moved quickly past the reception desk and lunchroom into the first greenhouse.

He stared at her unsurprised, arms crossed on his chest as he leaned against a bench. "What took you so long, Carey?" Cold irony edged his voice.

Carey wilted a little as his black eyes impaled her. She drew in a sharp, shallow breath, and summoned her confidence.

"I want to buy it back. Whatever Todd owes you. How dare you think you can manipulate my brother right out of his inheritance?"

"You've got the wrong man," Gavin cut in sharply. "Redgrave's the one to talk to. But I doubt he'll listen. If you had two lifetimes to work it off, you'd never rid yourself of debt to him."

Stunned, Carey stepped back. Gavin straightened, his taut physique more imposing than she remembered.

"Carey, when will you learn? You're no match for Redgrave and his ilk." His mouth curled derisively.

"You're just as bad then, Gavin Jack. You conspired against me, you set me up, and now you're just waiting to take over my business. My family has run that business for over fifty years, and it will take more than a sick gambling brother and an irreputable rose grower to do me in." Carey spat the words out angrily and reached for the door.

Gavin locked his iron grip on her shoulder and spun her around. "If you'd take the blinders off, you'd realize the whole deal is exactly the opposite of what you think. I told Todd to stay clear of Redgrave, but he wouldn't listen to me any more than he does to his older sister." His eyes darkened with concern. "Because of what Redgrave was willing to do to your brother, just to expand his own empire, I severed my ties with him.

He wanted me to be his right-hand man—merge my op eration with his in return for control of both businesses when he retires. When I saw just how ruthless he was, I told him the deal was off."

"So what?" Carey returned sharply. "You can't really expect me to believe that would make any difference since you'll be his son by marriage anyway." Carey yanked her shoulder free and strode toward the lunch-room exit.

Gavin reached the door before she did, blocking her retreat. "You actually believe I'd still marry Alissa? I only put up with her to keep business relations running smoothly with her father. Friday night, before I saw you, I told Alissa I was through with her for good."

Gavin's words continued to sweep over her. "Now go on. Get out of here. Haven't you got some place better to be on a Sunday morning?"

Chapter Eleven

Carey drove more slowly down the road leading to Stockport than she had on her way out of town. It was too late for church. Besides, with her emotions locked in turmoil over problems with Todd and discoveries about Gavin, her mind would have been anywhere but on the sermon.

She tried to sort through the developments that had occurred over the past few hours. Life at McIlwain Greenhouse wouldn't be the same with Winston Redgrave owning half the business. Presumably, someone hand-picked by Winston would manage his interest in the operation. No telling what that could mean in changes to her daily routine. Though the burdens of small business ownership had not been easy, she had enjoyed making her own decisions and not answering to others.

Carey pulled into her driveway. With heavy steps, she let herself in the front door. Emptiness and silence greeted her. She moved down the hall and surveyed Todd's room from his open door. No posters hung on his walls; no shoes draped with dirty socks cluttered the corner; no sign of him remained. The reality of Todd's break with Stockport slowly sank in.

Carey returned to the living room, removed her Bible from her mother's cherry table, and slumped on the sofa. She read for a long time from Psalms and found some measure of peace and tranquility. She prayed earnestly for guidance, that she might make the best of her business association with Winston Redgrave.

Occasionally, Carey's mind strayed to her days as a fulltime music teacher. They lacked the stress and complications she'd muddled through since her parents' deaths and her return to Stockport to run the florist business. Life seemed almost simple then, by comparison, and she only recaptured a taste of those earlier times when her guitar students came to the house on Wednesday mornings.

Never far from her thoughts, Gavin Jack's image leapt frequently to the front of her mind. Supposing he *had* severed his relationship with Redgrave, would he still deliver the roses each Wednesday morning, or would Redgrave want to drop Gavin as his supplier? Probably so if Gavin's break with Alissa was as abrupt as he claimed. Or had she simply dangled herself as bait in front of Gavin for her father's benefit, in which case she had used him just as he had used her?

All the ramifications of these interwoven factors would only become clear in time, but the various possibilities staggered Carey's imagination. She determined to stop worrying and deal with the situation a day at a time.

Carey arose from the sofa and called her cousin Gail to ask for help at the shop until the details with Redgrave could be settled.

Carey and Gail opened shop together at eight o'clock the following morning. Gail, apprehensive about handling the retail responsibilities while Maggie was on vacation, gradually gained confidence and returned from her lunch break to relieve Carey with a more optimistic attitude.

"I'll be fine for an hour, Carey. Just don't go ordering any seven course meal." Gail's amber eyes twinkled.

"If you'd like, you can start on the billing while I'm gone. That's an easy job to handle between customer interruptions." Carey showed Gail how to prepare the invoices for mailing, then walked home for lunch.

When Carey returned to the shop an hour later, Winston Redgrave and his daughter, Alissa, faced Gail over the front customer counter. Carey's stomach knotted.

"No wonder they're having difficulties, Father. Look at this. They don't have the slightest idea how to price for profit." Alissa pointed to an invoice Gail had prepared.

Gail, red-faced and flustered, motioned to Carey the moment she stepped through the side door.

"Mr. Redgrave, I've been expecting you." Carey offered her hand, ignoring Alissa entirely. Winston Redgrave's handshake was hearty and genuine.

"We've just come from the bank, Carey. Alissa and I have straightened out all the technicalities to install her in your brother's place until the final paperwork is drawn up by my lawyer. Todd told you, I presume." Winston Redgrave's smile softened his imposing image very little.

"Todd said he'd sold to you, but he didn't mention Alissa." Carey straightened, squaring her shoulders, hoping it would strengthen her image. She needed any advantage she could give herself in dealing with the Redgraves.

"Well, here I am, ready to put your house in order." Alissa's cool, authoritative manner rankled. "First, I think I'll introduce a new pricing structure for your retail products. Don't stuff any more of those into envelopes," she ordered Gail. "Starting right now, I'll take care of all the billing." Alissa jogged Gail's stack of invoices into a neater pile.

"If you're taking over for Todd, your job is back there." Carey pointed to the greenhouses. "I'd suggest you find something else to wear unless you don't mind potting soil all over your expensive outfit," Carey explained with perfect control. She was inwardly amused at the image of Alissa, in her designer clothes, manicured nails, and heavy makeup, doing Todd's work in the greenhouse.

"Daddy, I think you'd better explain to Carey just who calls the shots around here, as in, who owns controlling interest." Alissa raised one brow poignantly.

"I'm really sorry you hadn't been told," Redgrave began. "Since I paid off the entire balance on the fifteen-thousand-dollar loan taken out for Todd's previous gambling debt, I now hold controlling interest in McIlwain Greenhouses. It was the one bargaining factor your brother insisted upon, not wanting to leave you in debt when he parted with his share in the family business. Rather considerate of him, I thought, to be so concerned for your future."

A young mother with two small children entered the shop, and browsed at the planters and arrangements along the front shelves.

"Mr. Redgrave, could we meet at a different time and place to iron out the details of your recent acquisition? If you and your daughter could give me until tomorrow morning, I'm sure we can agree on a suitable working arrangement. I'd be happy to come to your office at, say, nine o'clock?"

Winston Redgrave's mouth cracked into a wry smile. The slow blinking of his left eye told Carey he read perfectly the underlying implications in her remark. He extracted his business card and handed it to Carey. "I'll see you at nine sharp. Alissa, shall we go?" He eyed her sharply.

Her face fell with disappointment, but she dared not counter her father. Reluctantly, she left the stack of invoices on the counter and followed him out the door.

Carey stood watching the two leave and trying to digest this latest blow, while Gail moved to help the customer. Gavin's assessment had proved more accurate than Carey had imagined in her wildest dreams. Knowing Redgrave could buy and sell McIlwain Greenhouses many times over, Carey accepted the fact that he'd probably never let go of the portion he now held claim to. But she also knew she could dangle her share of the business in front of him like a carrot—and she could make it a much more expensive carrot than he'd purchased from her brother.

Carey worked well into the night preparing for her encounter with the Redgrave duo. She drew up a list of bargaining points, in order of priority, and hoped to come away with as much of the list intact as possible. At nine the next morning, she sat across from Winston Redgrave in his office. He made an initial offer to buy the whole business, then Carey countered with her own proposal.

"I'll consider your offer under these conditions. Maggie and Floyd Emery remain employees, their duties outlined here, until retirement or resignation. You pick up one hundred percent of their life insurance, health and dental insurance and allow them each four weeks paid vacation per year, plus the ten paid holidays listed." Carey met Winston, eyeball to eyeball.

"You've thought of everything, haven't you?" The corner of Winston Redgrave's mouth moved upward like that of a shrewd businessman enjoying the heat of negotiations.

"It's too much, if you ask me," Alissa interrupted.

"Which I didn't. You'd do well to remember who pays your allowance," Winston chided his daughter. "Carey, I see nothing at all wrong with what you're asking. I'd have done the same myself. For that, you have my respect. I'll have the papers drawn up this week and meet with you at the lawyer's office on Friday afternoon to close the deal. That will give you the rest of this week to prepare the shop for new management on Monday morning."

"Daddy! Aren't you even going to horsetrade? 'You keep the truck, the Emerys have to go,' sort of thing?" Alissa whined.

"Absolutely not. The Emerys know that business inside out. Their help will prove invaluable to you. I'm sorry you haven't the maturity to realize that experience is extremely valuable in this business, something which, right now, you're sadly lacking." Alissa's only response was a silent pout.

"You'd better start eating that humble pie, daughter, because I'm putting Mrs. Emery in charge of the retailing as soon as she returns from vacation, and you'll do as she asks, or you can forget about your fancy car, your credit cards, and everything else that's in my name."

Carey mustered every ounce of self-control to refrain from gloating. "It's been interesting to deal with you, Mr. Redgrave. You've made it as painless as possible. My worst fears over the process never materialized."

"You didn't know this, Carey, but I asked your folks to sell me that operation years ago. Of course, your parents wouldn't hear of it as long as Todd planned to come into the business some day. But since he was the first to express a desire to sell, I had to strike while the iron was hot." Winston showed Carey to the door.

"Until Friday, then." Carey shook his hand and left.

The bargaining process with Redgrave had gone smoothly, but it renewed Carey's uneasiness about Gavin's involvement with Redgrave and Todd. Redgrave made his deal sound so innocent, but Carey knew him to be cunning and cold-hearted. He took advantage of Todd's weakness, just like someone offering a recovering alcoholic a glass of whiskey. Todd had no will of his own to turn the money down, and Redgrave knew it.

Carey had hammered out a good deal for herself financially. Maybe Redgrave had felt some guilt over his less-than-honorable methods and for this reason had given her the figure she had asked, but Carey doubted it.

By Thursday afternoon, Carey and Gail had prepared the shop and greenhouses well for the change in ownership. Carey worked in the back most of the time, straightening the storage area and taking inventory. She wrote out a complete crop schedule in legible printing. Her personal schedule, scribbled onto the squares of a calendar, was legible only to herself.

Carey noticed that her attitude had shifted completely concerning her desire to preserve the family business. The idea of selling to Redgrave didn't cause the mountains of anguish it had only a few days earlier when she had confronted Gavin in his greenhouse. Keeping McIlwain Greenhouses seemed a valiant, yet futile goal, considering the events since October.

How ironic that Todd, the one for whom the business had been preserved, turned out to be the least interested and least capable of maintaining it. Carey felt it had been folly for her to knock herself out to carry the business successfully. But she would make the same choice if she had to do it over again. For some reason, known only to the Lord, it simply wasn't meant to be.

Another turning point in her life had arrived. After Friday, she would seek another full-time teaching position. A few weeks remained before September and school. Carey hoped some music teacher would have a last minute change of plans and create a vacant position. The chance was slim.

On Friday morning, Carey faced Winston across a mahogany table in a conference room on the fourth floor of a Rochester law office.

"I'll need your signature here, and here, Ms. McIlwain." Carey complied, returning the pen to Mr. Gordon, the attorney presiding at the closing. "That completes the legalities. Here's your check, Ms. McIlwain." The bespectacled gentleman looked from Carey to Winston. "You may use this room as long as you like for any last minute discussion." He closed the door quietly behind him.

"What are your plans from here, Carey? Not that you need to worry. With what I just paid you for your share of McIlwain Greenhouses, you could afford the luxury of time to decide." Winston Redgrave regarded her with curiosity.

"I'll go back to teaching music at the earliest possible opportunity. It's my real love," Carey explained. "I expect you'll keep your eagle eye open for more opportunities to expand your business. Soon you'll be the only retailer in the county," Carey exaggerated.

"You flatter me," Winston smiled. "Actually, I can't afford many more deals like this one. You've cost me more than you know. Price tag aside, Gavin Jack canceled our agreement to combine operations when he learned I'd bought your brother's share. That hurt me badly." Winston leaned forward. "Gavin claimed I took advantage of your brother's gambling problem to ruthlessly expand my business. Gavin's a man of much higher principle than I gave him credit for."

Winston's words twisted a dagger inside Carey. Gavin had been telling her the truth after all, when he said he'd opposed Winston's offer to Todd. And she had accused Gavin of precisely the opposite, of conspiring against her.

"No, Carey, I should have believed Gavin." Winston continued. "I'd have never gone through with my offer to Todd if I'd thought it would cost me the Jack Brothers deal. I just figured, like anyone else, Gavin had his price, but I was wrong. No matter what I offered, he stood by his convictions." Regret showed clearly in his eyes. Winston checked his watch, then rose. "Good luck, Carey."

"Thank you." She stood and offered her hand.

Carey deposited most of her payment from Winston into a special high-interest checking account in a nearby bank. Next she headed for a downtown jewelers.

Late Sunday afternoon, Carey pulled into the Emerys' driveway behind their camper. Maggie greeted her on the screened front porch of their older two-story, white frame home.

"How was your trip? You didn't send me a card," Carey accused, hugging Maggie.

"By golly, you're right. They didn't have cards where we went. I'll just blame it on Floyd," she winked. "He insisted on a wilderness campsite somewhere in the middle of the Adirondacks."

"What's that? Did I hear my name?" Floyd joined them on the porch. "Don't believe her, Carey. We must've had a dozen opportunities to buy postcards. She came home with a whole stack for the album."

Carey laughed at the admonishing look Maggie shot

at Floyd. "The postcard isn't important. Did you have a good time?"

"Fabulous. Caught the biggest trout you'd ever care to see," Floyd explained. "Must have been a full two pounds heavier than the biggest one I got last year!"

"You old storyteller," Maggie scolded.

Carey grinned at the playfulness between the older couple, despite their nearly thirty-five years of marriage. For all but eleven of their married years, they had worked for McIlwain Greenhouses, which made the news she had come to tell them even more difficult to share.

"Now, what brings you for a visit on Sunday afternoon, Carey? You look like you have something important on your mind." Floyd half smiled as he tamped his pipe.

Carey reached inside her bag and removed two oblong boxes, carefully gift-wrapped, with small notecards attached. "I've been trying to think of an easy way to say this," she began, holding back the lump threatening to close off her thoat, "but there isn't any." She handed each a box. Fighting hard to keep back tears, she forced herself to smile. "Maggie, Floyd, you've worked for McIlwain Greenhouses for nearly twenty-five years, but come Monday morning, you'll have to decide whether you'll work for a new owner."

Floyd set his pipe aside. "Well," he drawled, "this *is* big news."

"I suspected something was up." Maggie spoke quietly. "But sentimental as I am, I was hoping for a different kind of news." She lowered her eyes, fidgeting nervously with the bow on her package.

Carey continued uncomfortably. "Last week Todd sold his share of the business to Winston Redgrave of Redgrave Greenhouses in Rochester. When I learned

Todd's future plans didn't include taking over the business, and then discovered the difficulties involved in co-ownership with the Redgraves, I decided to sell my share to Redgrave also, with restrictions."

Carey outlined the benefit plan Redgrave had agreed to for the Emerys. Floyd's brow lifted noticeably when he learned of his four-weeks paid vacation yearly, and Carey could see the wheels turning as he imagined which trout streams he'd try next year.

When she explained that Alissa Redgrave would be working under Maggie in the shop, a mischievous look glinted in Maggie's eyes, and Carey knew with assurance that Alissa would be in for the experience of her life.

"I couldn't let our association end without giving you a small gift of appreciation—something to remember the McIlwain family by." Carey watched as the Emerys opened their gifts.

Maggie removed hers from her box first. She held up the gold watch, studded by a circle of diamonds around its face. "Carey, it's lovely. But far too expensive. I couldn't—"

"Yes, you can," Carey interrupted. "I'll be crushed if you don't keep it and wear it."

"How'd you know mine quit on me not two weeks ago?" Floyd asked. "Thanks, Carey. This is the fanciest timepiece I've ever owned." Floyd slipped his watch on his wrist.

"No, you don't, buster. That isn't for everyday," Maggie informed him. "You get yourself one of those five-dollar cheapies for work and save that one for special."

"Yes, ma'am," Floyd conceded reluctantly. He admired his watch, then laid it back in its box.

"What about you, Carey?" Maggie asked.

"I'm going to look for another teaching job," she answered.

"Good luck, Carey, and you be sure to keep in touch."

Carey rose to leave. "I promise. Good luck to you both. Especially to you, Maggie, training Alissa." Carey hugged Maggie, then Floyd.

"I'll be sure and take my mean pills tomorrow," Maggie joked. "No uppity socialite is going to get my goat."

"That's the spirit. Take care now." Carey slid behind the wheel of her old rusty Mustang and waved as she backed out of the driveway.

Chapter Twelve

On Monday morning, Carey compiled a list of local school systems and phone numbers, then began calling. If she could find a job locally, she could continue living in the McIlwain home.

After two hours, she had turned up no music openings. Several systems invited Carey to put her name on the substitute teacher list. With Rochester nearby, she could probably be as busy as she wanted doing substitute work, but that didn't interest her.

Carey stared at the long list of potential jobs she had crossed out one by one. Then another thought came to her. She dialed again.

"Marilee, this is Carey."

"Carey? I can't believe it!" her former teaching roommate exclaimed. "We haven't talked since Christmas. How are you? How's the florist business? Fill me in on everything. Met any interesting men lately?"

Carey answered some of Marilee's questions and avoided others, knowing she couldn't easily explain anything about the men in her life. She eventually brought the conversation around to her reason for calling.

"Marilee, have you heard of any music openings

nearby? I've scoured this entire area, and all I can come up with is subbing."

"There might be one right here. The teacher Mr. Ackerman hired to replace you last fall didn't like living in the hills. I don't know if Mr. Ackerman's found someone else to take the job, but I'm sure he'd love to have you back. Oh, Carey, if you moved back to Harrington, we'd have a riot!"

Carey grew excited at the possibility of returning to the position she had enjoyed so much. She called Mr. Ackerman right away. He said the job was open and hers for the taking. Carey accepted immediately and then placed another call to Marilee to make plans to move in.

Carey decided to leave Stockport on the following Sunday afternoon. Throughout the week, she packed her belongings and prepared to close up the house.

On Friday Carey left the house soon after lunch and drove toward Rochester. Besides wishing to make a withdrawal from her checking account at the bank there, she wanted to do some shopping. She decided that, before moving back to the hills, back to the semi-isolation of Harrington, she should treat herself to a last-minute fling in the downtown department stores.

The display windows featured the fall lines of all her favorite sportswear. Split skirts in muted gray-and-blue plaids, angora-blend sweaters in coordinating tones, and blazers for every occasion and in many fabrics abounded.

School clothes, outerwear, boots, and bags beckoned to her from the showcases. Carey wandered first through B. Foreman, her favorite store of all. Their first-floor shoe department, one where Carey frequently shopped when in Rochester, offered fashionable heels as well as flats. She tried on several pairs, and decided on black, round-toed flats for school, plus high-heeled sandals in taupe for dressier occasions.

In sportswear, Carey tried on wool blazers, searching for the exact fit and color to complement outfits she'd bought last year. One, in Irish tweed, contained the muted federal blue tone of her favorite wool slacks. Another, this one a plaid, brought out the delicate buff of her pleated skirt.

Sweaters caught Carey's eye next. A pointelle in pale yellow fit perfectly. She couldn't resist a long-sleeved, natural-white, party sweater with a crocheted yoke. The lacy pattern dipped into a V in front and back. She also bought another after-hours concoction, this one a wrap dress in white with charcoal-gray trim.

On her way out of the store, Carey passed the scarf display. She riffled through the myriad of colors and patterns hanging from the chrome circle. One, in aqua, black, and beige stripes, looked perfect for Marilee. She asked the clerk to wrap it in a gift box.

The excursion lifted Carey's spirits immeasurably. When she stashed her new purchases into the trunk of her car, she imagined the cool crisp air of October evenings to come—the football games on Friday nights, the crunch of leaves beneath her feet, and the indescribable array of autumn colors, which would paint the hills visible from her apartment bedroom window.

Carey took a route to the north of Rochester toward Stockton. She had driven the expressway into the city, but wanted variety on the way home. Her thoughts centered on the tasks to be completed in the short amount of time left before her move away.

High on the list of 'unfinished business' was her relationship with Gavin Jack. Not for the first time in recent days, her conscience troubled her over their last encounter. She should apologize to him in person for having wrongly accused him. He deserved to know that she realized he wasn't involved in Todd's selling to Redgrave.

Gavin would probably bask in her apology, but if she didn't try to set things right, the incident would ride on her conscience for weeks to come. Carey pulled up to a red light, her mind engrossed in what she should say to him. The car behind her honked when the light changed. She started up, then realized she wasn't far from the side road leading into Medeena.

Carey braced herself. This would be as good a time as any to face Gavin. Perhaps, late on a Friday afternoon, she might even find him in a good mood. She gripped her wheel and turned right at the next intersection. Several minutes later, she parked her rusty Mustang in front of the rose grower's office. When she tried the door, she found it locked.

In the distance, a sports car stood in the circular drive to the imposing white mansion. Carey shuddered at her recollection of Alissa and Gavin together, but realized Alissa's sports car had been red, not black like the one parked there now.

Perhaps the car belonged to Gavin. She hadn't gotten a good look at his car the night he confronted her on her front porch.

Carey slid back into her car and made her way up the long driveway, parking behind the sleek, low, black car. Her heart pounded in her ears as she mounted the steps to the massive, white, double doors. She couldn't remember what she had wanted to say and questioned her sanity at having come. Her finger poised over the doorbell.

Apprehension overcame her. Carey jammed her hand into her pocket and turned to leave. She heard the front door open, and a smooth, commanding voice.

"Carey, don't run away."

The words reverberated in her head. Carey froze, unwilling to face Gavin, but unable to walk away.

"I was right about you after all, wasn't I, Teacher?" Gavin's statement was unexpected and set her stomach churning.

Carey turned around. Her eyes locked on Gavin's tall, powerful form, framed in the opening of one of the double doors. Her mind spun as she tried to form words into sentences. Gradually, she succeeded in organizing her thoughts.

"Yes. You were right. I am a teacher." She gained confidence at the sound of her own, clear voice. With a sense of conviction, Carey spoke the words she had come to say.

"I apologize for accusing you wrongly. I know now that you tried to discourage Winston Redgrave from buying Todd out." She watched his eyes, at first hard and unreadable, soften with some indefinable emotion.

Carey waited for him to speak, but silence spanned the distance between them. She awkwardly cast her eyes downward and turned to leave.

"Carey, don't go." His words were half command, half plea. She stopped momentarily, her pulse racing.

Gavin turned her toward him, his strong grip warm upon her shoulders. He scrutinized her face, as if some well-hidden secret lay waiting for him there.

Musky cologne filled her with a sweet, heady sensation, then Carey found herself locked willingly in Gavin's embrace. He brought her to him, claiming her lips, spinning her senses into a patternless orbit. Their hearts beat a syncopated duet as Carey returned Gavin's kiss. Long moments later, the kiss ended.

"Carey, you can't know how many times I've wanted to do that." Gavin's thick, husky words sent a shiver through her.

Gavin's desire and her own responses to him made her tremble. Again, his demanding lips caressed hers.

As Gavin's affections sent new spirals of delight through her, warning bells sounded in the far recesses of Carey's mind. Slowly, her responses to his touch gave way to apprehension, and she pressed forcefully against his chest to escape his embrace.

Stunned, Gavin faltered, stepping back. Shock and incomprehension contorted his features.

"What's the matter, Carey?" His words had an edge of concern she had never heard from him before.

Carey felt defensive and unsure of herself. "I pulled away from you for a reason you may never understand."

"Carey, you've shown up on my doorstep uninvited. You willingly returned my kiss. Now, you say I'll never understand. What does it take to get the message through to you, Carey? I care about you! Don't waste yourself on someone you don't love. You'll regret it for a lifetime."

"How can you know about love—or about me?" she challenged.

"I know what you're saying when I kiss you." The truth hit Carey like a thundering blow. She'd given away far too much of her feelings for him.

Carey spun around and ran down the steps toward her car. Gavin followed, catching her by the arm, pulling her up against him. She stared into his emotion-darkened eyes.

"Marry the old plant doctor, if that's what you want, but just remember, you had your chance at real love, and you ran away from it." Swiftly, he released her and disappeared inside his mansion.

Carey's hand shook as she turned her key in the ignition. Somehow, she maneuvered the Mustang toward Stockport with very little conscious effort on her part.

Totally distracted, she kept hearing Gavin's admonition over and over again. "You had your chance at real love, and you ran away from it." How could he know? Was he telling her that he loved her?

She couldn't admit to Gavin that she already agreed with his conclusion about Alex. What she felt for Alex belonged in a different category from the emotion she felt for Gavin. Yet Carey wanted Gavin to believe she planned her future with Alex. It bought her time to think, to figure out exactly what this exciting, yet troublesome feeling for Gavin meant.

If Gavin cared for her as he claimed, he wouldn't let her go easily, of this she was certain. She had come to him enough times in the past; now it would be up to him.

Carey unloaded her purchases from the trunk of the car and carried them into her bedroom. Too tired to cook and too upset to eat, Carey boiled water for tea and sought solace in prayer and Scripture. She asked the Lord to guide her, as always, so that her future plans would be His will for her life. Once again she found comfort in David's words from the Psalms. They soothed her troubled heart as she imagined his harp playing had done for Saul. She felt better, knowing she had made her apology to Gavin, and prayed that he would come to know God's love.

On Sunday afternoon, Carey packed the last of her belongings into the Mustang. She drove across town to the Emerys'. They were expecting her and waved from their front porch as she parked in their driveway.

"How about some lemonade before you go?" Maggie asked, holding the porch door open.

"No, thank you, Maggie. I can't stay long." Carey took a seat on the padded lounge.

"Not a bad day for driving," Floyd commented, peering at the sky through the front screens. "They're predicting rain for late afternoon. How long will you be on the road?"

"Four hours," Carey answered. "I expect to arrive for dinner. I'm really looking forward to seeing my roommate again. Marilee and I became good friends, but you know how it is when miles come between."

"Speaking of miles coming between, have you heard from Todd?" Maggie inquired.

"No, I haven't. Please let me know if you hear anything here, Maggie. Todd hasn't contacted me, but I believe he'll return to Stockport after he's made progress dealing with his problem. I've left a note for him at the house. He'll know how to reach me if he shows up there."

"You know, Carey, for a while I was afraid Gavin Jack had gotten mixed up with the wrong crowd, but he's sure gained my respect. I used to think he was a hoodlum of sorts. Now I know how wrong I was." Maggie's unprompted admission surprised Carey.

"What makes you say that?" Carey arched her brow in question.

"Working with the Redgrave girl." Maggie's eyes rolled upward. "Anything she says, I just take the opposite point of view, and figure I'll come out close to right. From the way she's badmouthed Gavin—all because he wouldn't play ball with her father—I've got to give the man credit. He really tried to save your family's business. He just didn't stand a chance with two Redgraves and a Todd McIlwain against him."

"I always liked Gavin Jack," Floyd put in. He set his pipe aside. "He got into his share of mischief as a youngster. I don't mean he was perfect, but he was a good boy. Helped with that rose growing business from the time he was a little kid. Was his father ever proud of him the day he went into the army!" The reminiscing brought a faraway look to Floyd's eyes.

"You know, Carey," Maggie began, "there's something you ought to be proud of, and that's the way you've handled the flower shop since your parents' accident. You picked right up on that business and did all right when the money was tight, too."

Carey dropped her eyes. Maggie's compliment brought a lump to her throat. When she looked up again, tiny tears clung to her eyelashes. "I appreciate your telling me that, Maggie."

"Maggie's not just saying that to hear herself talk, either," Floyd put in. "I agree with her one hundred percent."

"Oh, Floyd," she went to him and kissed his cheek.

"Now give me a hug before you go," Maggie said. "Then you'd best get on the road, or you'll be late arriving in Harrington."

Carey hugged Maggie then checked her watch. Already, it said half past two. She reached into her purse, extracted a slip of paper and handed it to Maggie. "This is my Harrington address. I expect you to write to me. And call me collect if you learn anything about Todd."

Maggie and Floyd saw Carey out.

"You drive carefully, you hear?" Floyd cautioned.

"I will," Carey promised, remembering her parents' accident.

Carey drove south toward route 490, the New York state thruway, which would take her across the state to Syracuse and Interstate 81.

The thruway leg of the journey passed across flat terrain, and driving this stretch of road generally presented no challenge. Carey relaxed as she listened to her car radio.

An hour east of Rochester, rain sprinkled her windshield. Dark clouds moved overland from Lake Ontario to the north and the breeze picked up.

The rain gradually increased. Carey switched her windshield wipers to the highest speed. The blades slapped water away in rhythmic sheets, but Carey had to strain to see the road. She gripped her wheel more securely and leaned forward for a better view.

A trailer truck pulled alongside Carey in the left lane. Carey moved to the right of her own lane to give the truck driver more room. Several cars strung out ahead of her with no break.

Suddenly, torrents of rain pelted her windshield in waves, decreasing her visibility. The truck alongside her speeded up, throwing a rooster tail of water at her. Carey panicked. She could no longer see the car which had been no more than thirty feet in front of her. She carefully applied her brakes. Unexpectedly, the car hydroplaned, fishtailing across to the left lane, then back toward the shoulder. Icy fear gripped her heart.

Carey pumped her brakes. The taillights of the car in front loomed at her. She pulled on her steering wheel to avoid a collision and overcompensated. Her right tires dropped from the pavement to soft gravel. Her heart raced as she struggled for control. The rear end swung farther off the road. Roadside reflectors crashed against her car making her stomach churn with nausea. She jammed her brakes to the floor. The Mustang spun to a halt facing the oncoming traffic. Carey sat, numb with shock.

"Thank You, Lord," she whispered.

Carey's cold, clammy hands trembled uncontrollably. Someone knocked on her window.

"You all right?" An older gentleman with silver hair stood in the rain, his drenched shirt clinging to his chest.

"I'm O.K., thanks," she replied.

"I've got a CB. I'll call the troopers," he offered, then ran back to his car.

Carey rummaged in the back seat for an umbrella. She stepped out into the downpour to survey the damage to her car. Miraculously, she hadn't hit any other cars, only the reflector signs lining the thruway.

The right-rear quarter panel sustained heavy damage. She thanked the Lord for preventing her from hitting other vehicles.

Carey got in her car and waited. The state troopers arrived a few minutes later, took a report, then directed her back into the flow of traffic.

The rain continued until Carey neared the turnoff on Interstate 81 to route 17 at Binghamton. The scenic beauty increased as she traveled eastward through the rolling hills near the Catskills. Gradually, sunshine peaked from behind fluffy clouds.

Less than an hour later, Carey turned off route 17 into the tiny village of Harrington.

Chapter Thirteen

Nothing seemed to have changed in Harrington since the previous October when she had left so hurriedly for her parents' funeral. Her favorite old gas station on the corner of Main and Oak Streets piled stacks of tires out front supporting signs about the latest special.

Carey turned right in the center of town and followed Smith Street over the bridge spanning the Delaware River. At that point she technically entered Pennsylvania, although some students rode buses across the state line to attend Harrington Central.

A quarter of a mile from the bridge stood the home where she shared an apartment with Marilee. It was a tall, white, older house sitting on a hill overlooking the river. The spacious second floor apartment included two bedrooms, a generous living room and kitchen, and a bathroom. Their elderly, spinster landlady, Lucy Welch, treated them more like granddaughters than tenants.

Carey backed into the driveway and parked as close to the front door as possible. The moment she stepped from her car, Marilee burst out the front door.

"Carey, it's great to see you." Marilee, a scant five feet tall, stretched on tiptoe to hug Carey.

"It's great to be here. In one piece, I might add." Carey pointed to the side of her Mustang.

"What happened, kid?" Marilee's pale-blue eyes surveyed the damage to Carey's car. "You didn't get hurt, did you?"

Carey shook her head. "The car took the worst of it from those reflector posts along the thruway. I hit a bad rainstorm and spun off the road."

"That's a terrible shame." Marilee's head moved slowly from side to side. "I know a good body shop if you need one. Dave's Body Shop fixed mine last winter."

"I'll call my insurance company tomorrow. I doubt this car is worth fixing. Maybe I'll have to get a new one."

"Lucky you. I love shopping for new cars, but that day won't come for me for a very long time. I'm up to my eyebrows in payments on that one." Marilee pointed to her T-top Camaro. "Enough of this chatter. Lucy is anxious to see you. I'll bet she's got our spaghetti almost ready."

"She invited us to dinner and made my favorite?" Carey asked, already tasting the rich tomato sauce.

Marilee nodded. "My diet goes down the drain tonight all because of you. But I want you to know I've lost five pounds since I saw you last."

"Good for you."

"Before you say more, I also gained it all back plus another pound. I wish I were naturally slim like you. Actually, all I need is another four inches in height." Marilee wrinkled her nose. "I hate tall, slim people." She scowled playfully. Marilee hooked her arm through Carey's, chatting nonstop as they walked inside.

"Lucy, it smells scrumptious," Carey exclaimed as she rushed to hug the older woman.

"Carey, dear. It's so wonderful to have you back. Marilee needs your level-headed influence, I fear." Lucy Welch, a slender lady in her midseventies, kissed Carey's cheek.

"What's this about Marilee?"

"Wait until you see it." Lucy shook her head deliberately while she clicked her tongue. "She's gone daffy upstairs. But, if you like her doings up there, then I guess it's O.K."

"What's she talking about?" Carey regarded Marilee curiously.

"Later, kid." Marilee winked. "Let's eat. I'm starving."

During dinner hour, Carey caught up on the latest Harrington news—marriages, teacher reassignments, rumors of resignations.

Miss Welch served her fabulous coconut cream pie for dessert.

"I haven't had a piece of this since the last time I ate with you. You haven't lost your touch, Lucy."

"Thank you, Carey. Now, before it gets any later, you two young ladies go ahead and unpack Carey's car. I'll take care of the cleanup."

Carey began stacking her dishes and carrying them to the sink.

"Go on, Carey." Lucy waved her hand in dismissal. "It'll be so good just to hear two pairs of feet upstairs again."

Marilee and Carey each grabbed an armload of belongings from the car and carted them up the stairs. "What's this 'daffy' thing Lucy was talking about?" Carey asked, as Marilee preceded her up the stairs.

"Hope you like it," Marilee said, swinging the apartment door wide open.

Inside, the color scheme of the apartment had changed from traditional antique ivory, to stark white with a rainbow mural painted on the largest wall of the living room. None of the hand-me-down furniture from Carey's days remained. New modular pieces in primary colors complimented the wall mural. Chrome, glass, and natural wood abounded. A coarse-weave area rug with large blocks of the same bright colors covered the hardwood floor.

"Marilee, I'm speechless." Carey carefully avoided any negative response. The drastic change, representing a substantial investment on Marilee's part, caught Carey off guard.

"You like this? Wait till you see your bedroom!"

Carey held her breath while Marilee opened the door. Against the same bright-white background, a mural of a musical staff and notes, again in bright primary colors, had been painted. "This is incredible, Marilee. What ever possessed you to make all these changes?"

"Remember Nick Sabrino?"

Carey nodded. Nick, the overzealous, five-foot-four art teacher, never lacked for ambitious plans.

"He does interior design during the summer. Isn't his work just…" Marilee shrugged her shoulders excitedly.

"I'm like you, Marilee—at a loss for words." Carey laid her garment bag on her bed and stood back. The new decor would take some getting used to.

Carey settled in during the next several days. The homey feeling she remembered in the apartment had disappeared with its new, contemporary decorating scheme and furnishings.

A good deal of her time was taken with her wrecked car. Carey contacted her insurance company. She sent them an estimate of the damages, and they forwarded her a check for the value of her seven-year-old Mustang. She shopped with the local car dealer for another car, but postponed making a decision.

Even Marilee had changed considerably. Nick Sabrino dropped by constantly. Although neither admitted to more than friendship, Carey noticed the starry look in Marilee's eyes when she spoke of Nick and the affectionate way they related to one another.

Not a day went by that Carey didn't think about Gavin Jack. Seeing Marilee and Nick together brought him constantly to mind. She thought she had left that part of her past behind when she drove away from Stockport, but memories are no respecter of geographical locations.

In the last two days before school opened, Carey prepared her band room for the start of school. The band library, difficult to keep in order, needed hours of attention. Some of the school instruments required minor repair, such as pad replacements on clarinets. She decorated her bulletin boards with colorful instrument posters.

Preliminary teacher meetings reunited Carey with the staff she had come to respect. Mr. Ackerman, the superintendent of the small school system, gave her such a hearty welcome that Carey wondered about the music teacher who had taken her place and then resigned the position after one year.

After two weeks of school, Carey's instrumental music lesson schedule had settled into place. A few band rehearsals showed how little students had practiced over the summer months. The prospect of reshaping the junior band into a respectable ensemble challenged Carey, and sometimes she caught herself wondering what Gavin would think of her young charges.

Several guitar students from past years approached her about resuming private lessons, and Carey scheduled them at the end of the school day. It was often past five o'clock when she switched off the lights and started back to the apartment.

One Friday afternoon late in October, Carey was straightening band chairs and stands, tidying her music room before the weekend. A melancholy feeling gripped her. Her parents had died exactly one year ago.

Yet Carey blamed more than the anniversary of their deaths for her sadness. Gavin had weighed constantly on her mind in recent days. His frequent invasion of her thoughts grated on her nerves, causing her mind to wander when she needed to be concentrating on her teaching.

That one man could disturb her life so, even in his absence, forced Carey to reevaluate her priorities for happiness. Once, she believed she could lead a complete, fulfilled life with a career alone. Now she had returned to teaching only to find Gavin persistently intruding in her private domain. She began to question whether music teaching alone could sustain her emotionally.

Carey glanced at the wall clock. Already it was past five-thirty. Through the open band-room door her eyes caught some movement. Carey's breath caught in her lungs. In the darkened hallway, she saw the image of Gavin Jack. Questioning her sanity, Carey promised herself a weekend of rest and resolved anew to banish all thoughts of the man.

When she had straightened the last chair and stand, Carey grabbed her coat from the closet and draped it over her arm. She locked the band-room door, switched out the lights, and latched the door behind her. A figure stepped from the shadows of the dimly lit hall. Carey gasped in terror.

"Working overtime, Carey?" came the low, smooth tone.

"Gavin? What are you doing here?" Carey asked, her weak voice trembling.

"I came to see you." Tenderness characterized his simple statement, tearing at Carey's heart.

The small amount of natural light filtering into the hallway silhouetted Gavin's tall, rugged form, triggering all the old excitement Carey had experienced in past encounters. She stood, still somewhat dazed, as Gavin removed her coat from her arm and helped her slip it on.

"My car's right outside," he explained, his hand behind her back as he moved with her toward the end of the hall. "Can we talk?"

"Gavin, why did you come here to see me?" she implored. She couldn't believe he was actually here walking beside her.

"Because I've learned something important about myself over the past several weeks, and I need to share it with you." Gavin held the door open. Outside, the chilling October breeze nipped at them in the fading daylight. His black sports car was parked a few feet away.

"We could talk at my apartment, if you'd rather," Carey suggested.

"Will we have any privacy? Now that I've come, I don't want to share you with anyone—at least not until I say my piece." Gavin held her eyes with his black, compelling gaze.

"We'll have privacy, at least starting about seven o'clock. My roommate has a date for the football game," Carey explained.

"Why don't I take you out for something to eat while we're waiting for your roommate to disappear?"

Carey, usually half starved by the end of the school day, had forgotten her hunger until Gavin's mention of dinner. "That sounds like a good strategy," she replied.

Gavin helped her into his car, then climbed behind the wheel. With Carey's directions, he drove toward her favorite restaurant in a neighboring town.

Kandy's Korner, a place Carey had discovered just this fall, offered neither an intimate atmosphere nor gourmet cuisine, just good, down-home cooking. In fact, it wasn't until the hostess had seated them that Carey realized how much it reminded her of Polly's Place, where Gavin had taken her for lunch following New Years.

For a while, Gavin kept conversation light, commenting on the natural beauty of the area and other topics equally devoid of controversy. He seemed so different, yet so like the Gavin she remembered—his good qualities amplified, the toughness smoothed away.

When they had nearly finished dessert, a contemplative look stole over his features.

"Carey, I want to tell you about something before we go to your apartment." He crumpled his paper napkin, then set it aside and looked directly at her. "Breaking my ties with Redgrave has turned out better than I thought. I knew it would be rough, but I tried out the idea on that paper you read beside the door in the greenhouse. If Redgrave wasn't going to be my partner, I needed the same 'Silent Partner' my folks had when times were hard for them. God has stayed with me, and the prosperity I now have is due to Him. It's a good feeling—to be putting my faith in God rather than myself."

"Gavin, I'm so happy for you," she managed, her voice hoarse with emotion. *Thank you, thank you, thank you, Lord!* she silently prayed.

They returned to the school for Carey's car, and Gavin followed her to her apartment.

As they came inside, Gavin presented Carey with a

161

large square box. "I brought along a little something for you."

Eagerly, she lifted the top flap. Inside was a cranberry glass bowl overflowing with tiny scarlet sweetheart roses.

"Oh, Gavin," her voice took on a breathy quality, "they're so beautiful." She placed them on an end table.

Gavin settled on the bright red couch while Carey started the coffeemaker. When she joined him in the living room, she curled her stockinged feet beneath her on a boxy chair diagonally across from Gavin. Carey caught herself blinking and staring, unadjusted still to the fact that Gavin had come to Harrington to see her.

"I've had a tough private struggle since we last saw one another, Carey. I told myself you didn't matter that much to me, that you were just someone I had felt sorry for and what you did with your life shouldn't affect mine." He leaned toward her, adding poignancy to his words. "But I never succeeded in convincing myself of that."

In the momentary silence that followed, Carey visually caressed the strongly carved lines of his face. The compelling look in his dark clear eyes captured her heart. She knew his statement had cost him a great emotional price.

"Carey," he paused, searching for exactly the right phrasing, "for weeks I've asked myself why I let you get away. After the last time I saw you, I was angry. I thought you'd decided to take up with that plant doctor, but I learned a few days later it wasn't true. Then I was mad at you for letting me believe it, when what you'd really done was come back here to teach. I've put myself through a lot of grief these last few weeks trying to forget about you, yet wondering if you'd give me a chance to show you how much I care."

Carey listened in stunned silence, shocked to learn Gavin had suffered the same anguish as she had over their parting, anguish that intensified for them both with the passing of time.

Gavin stood, pacing nervously to the window. Carey sensed he had interpreted her quietness as rejection. Swiftly, she joined him, touching his tense jawline with her fingertip.

"Oh, Gavin, I'm so glad you came." She spoke tenderly. "I've tried to put you out of my mind, but the harder I worked at it, the more impossible it became."

Carey watched a look of indescribable relief spread across his features as he gathered her into his embrace. He covered her face with kisses, at first rapid and light, then warm and lingering against her lips. Long moments later, Gavin shuddered and moaned before breaking the contact.

"Did you say you were making coffee?" Gavin asked, his voice husky. "I think we need it." He dropped a kiss on her nose.

Carey smiled to herself. "I'm sure it's ready by now."

In the kitchen alone, Carey hummed while finding mugs, napkins, and spoons for the serving tray. Her spirits soared to the heavens knowing Gavin had struggled, as she had, to erase the past, yet found it impossible. She stepped into the bathroom just off the kitchen to freshen her makeup and brush her hair, then carried the tray of coffee to the table in front of the couch.

Gavin sipped from the mug she handed him and nodded his appreciation. "At least I know you can make good coffee." He set his mug on the tray and took hers from her hands.

"Tell me, Teacher, what do you have planned for tomorrow?" He set her mug aside and pulled her close with one arm around her shoulder.

Carey thought immediately of the songs she had planned to compose for her private guitar students. She realized she had allowed lesson plans to spill over into her weekend hours for lack of a more productive way to fill her time.

"My time is your time, Gavin. What do you have in mind?"

"How would you like to go to New York with me for the day? If we get an early start, I'm certain I can have you back here before midnight."

Carey's thoughts raced at the exciting prospect of spending an entire day with Gavin in New York. The drive from Harrington took less than two hours, so they could easily manage the schedule he suggested.

"Oh, Gavin, I'd love to go." Carey hoped her enthusiasm hadn't become too obvious.

They chatted a while longer, finishing their coffee and making plans for the next day. Gavin rose and carried the tray into the kitchen for her.

"If we plan an early start tomorrow, I'd better not keep you up late," he explained, rinsing the mugs. He rapidly surveyed the kitchen. "Where's your dishwasher?"

"Right here," Carey grinned, raising both hands. "I'll take care of these." She removed a mug from his hand.

Gavin wandered into the living room while Carey put the tray away. When she joined him near the front door, Gavin drew her into his arms, and Carey rested her cheek against his shoulder.

"This is harder than I thought, leaving you here." His words brushed against her ear. Gavin stroked the side of her head, enmeshing his fingers in a mass of auburn tresses. Gently, he pulled her head back to gaze into her eyes. A pensive look stole over his features, then his

164

mouth covered hers with urgency and hunger.

Carey's breathing came in a harsh, uneven pattern as Gavin's heart beat against hers. Locked tightly in his arms, Carey savored the blissful security Gavin's closeness offered. When he released her, an unwanted chill traveled through her.

"I'll pick you up at seven-thirty tomorrow morning. We'll eat breakfast out. Can you be ready?"

"I wouldn't miss it for the world," Carey replied softly.

"Good night." Gavin left quickly, as if not trusting himself to remain any longer.

Carey floated to her bedroom, the reality of Gavin's visit so euphoric she questioned whether she would sleep at all. Minutes after her head hit the pillow, however, she succumbed to pleasant visions of herself with him for the entire day to come.

Chapter Fourteen

The following morning, Carey awoke to the sound of her clock radio, refreshed and enthused. The early morning weather report predicted sunny skies and mild temperatures. Their drive through the Catskills at this time of year would provide scenic panoramas of indescribable fall colors.

Carey chose her outfit carefully. Her yellow pointelle sweater clung attractively, emphasizing her feminine figure. She zipped her gray wool split skirt, its color offering a pleasing contrast.

A vigorous brushing restored bouncy liveliness to her hair. Carey chose her all-weather coat from the closet and stood by the door waiting when Gavin arrived.

"Good morning, beautiful," he whispered, slipping his arm around her. His lips touched hers. "Sleep well?" he asked.

Gavin guided her down the stairs with his hand in the small of her back, then held the car door for her. He settled into the driver's seat and pulled away, turning onto route 17 just outside the village. As Carey had hoped, the morning sun highlighted the hills, intensifying nature's artwork, a vibrant blending of oranges, golds, reds, and greens.

166

In Liberty, they stopped for coffee and donuts, then proceeded toward the city, crossing the Hudson on the Tappan Zee Bridge.

Traffic thickened as they neared the city, and more than once, Carey caught herself involuntarily putting on the brakes, though she hoped Gavin hadn't noticed. Skillfully, Gavin maneuvered into a parking ramp in midtown Manhattan, and they headed for the incomparable shops on Fifth Avenue.

Nothing, in Carey's opinion, could match the excitement of walking the streets of New York. The big-city smells of diner-cooked food mingled with the everpresent mild exhaust vapors. The bustling current of traffic sounds, occasionally punctuated by that of tires screeching, wasn't the same anywhere else in the world.

They window-shopped the displays of Sak's Fifth Avenue, then went inside. Together they browsed casually through the first floor menswear and wandered toward women's millinery.

"Try this on." Gavin handed Carey a black felt hat with a broad brim. Carey stood before a mirror, adjusting the hat on the center of her head. She turned to Gavin.

"What do you think?" She grinned playfully, unused to wearing any hat at all.

"Close, but not quite. This is what I had in mind." Gavin moved the hat forward and cocked it over one eye. "Now, you look like a woman of mystery and intrigue."

Carey closed her eyes to thin slits and regarded Gavin suspiciously. Catching her reflection in the mirror, she commented, "I don't have red-enough lipstick or long-enough nails for that. Besides, I'm missing the cigarette holder and cigarette." She mimed taking a puff on an imaginary smoke.

"I guess you're a different kind of woman." Gavin removed the hat, and they moved on. From Sak's they strolled the avenue to Tiffany's. Gavin tightened his arm around Carey as they browsed the exquisite pieces in elegant display cases. The seemingly endless offering of pearl necklaces stretched for yards beneath glass at one counter. There were pearls with turquoise, pearls with jade, pearls with coral, and white pearls alternating with black in carefully arranged strands.

"Which do you like best?" Gavin prodded quietly, his mouth near her ear.

Carey surveyed the length of the display before answering, then pointed to the special display case on top of the counter. "I'd take that one in a minute," she winked, pointing at a pearl rope choker consisting of multiple twisted strands.

Gavin lifted one corner of his mouth with feigned contempt. "Not your style at all, Carey. Besides, I prefer diamonds to pearls." Carey's pulse skipped a beat at Gavin's implication.

When they had finished browsing in Tiffany's, Gavin suggested a horse-drawn Hansom cab ride through Central Park. On their way to the park, he purchased two Coney dogs from a street vendor. "Think this will tide you over until dinner? I've got something special planned, and I want you to have plenty of appetite."

At the Plaza entrance, on Central Park South, Gavin hired a cabbie for an hour's ride. The clicking of the horse's hooves against the pavement, the afternoon reflections of multicolored trees in the pond reminded Carey of a scene from some romantic movie. Gavin rested his arm on Carey's shoulders, and she couldn't help asking herself if the day were really real, or simply a product of her imagination.

Following the tour of Central Park, Gavin insisted they take a cab to the Empire State Building. Carey's stomach felt a trifle queasy as the elevator neared the observation tower on the 102nd floor.

"Are you O.K.? You look a bit peaked." Gavin increased his support of her as they stepped from the elevator.

"I'll be fine," she assured him, her voice much weaker than she expected. "My stomach got off on about the fiftieth floor," she joked halfheartedly.

"Let's get some fresh air," Gavin suggested, guiding her outside.

When she had breathed the outdoor air for a few minutes, Carey felt the color returning to her cheeks. Gavin inserted a coin into a telescope and insisted she take the first look.

New York's skyline, with its seemingly infinite skyscrapers, was fascinating. Carey trained the scope on the Hudson River. The World Trade Center came clearly into view.

Gavin took a turn at the telescope, then moved to the outer edge of the observation tower, gazing silently into the distance. Carey stood back, wondering what occupied Gavin's mind, yet unwilling to intrude on his solitary meditations. Gavin lowered his head, and Carey noticed that his eyes closed for several seconds. When he looked up at her, a perfect peace seemed to wash over his expression. Carey moved to his side.

"You know," he began quietly, "a lot of years went by when I turned away from my faith, the beliefs my father and my uncle held dear in their business. I came so close to throwing my lot in with the unscrupulous. Now I thank the Lord every day that I'm in the rose growing business."

Carey returned his smile Her heart filled with happiness knowing Gavin's faith had been renewed.

"I think that Coney dog deserves some reenforcements," Gavin suggested. "Can your stomach handle the elevator ride down?"

"It will have to. I'm not taking the stairs after the walking we've done already," Carey's tone implied more confidence than she possessed.

Gavin hailed a taxi, giving the driver the name of a street unfamiliar to Carey. The cabbie maneuvered confidently through narrow streets, changing lanes dozens of times, making Carey crazy with apprehension. Gavin enjoyed it all, laughing at her worry. Eventually, they pulled in front of a tall building. Gavin paid the cabbie his fare and a generous tip, then helped Carey out of the cab.

Inside the lobby, they rode the elevator to the top floor where they stepped out onto a plushly carpeted hallway. Carey's feet sank ankle deep into the pile as Gavin escorted her to a small restaurant.

"Reservations for two for Gavin Jack," he told the uniformed maitre d'. The head waiter showed them to a window table looking out over the Manhattan skyline. Though the evening was young, a few lights shimmered in the gray shades of dusk.

Carey faced Gavin across an elegantly set table. A crystal bud vase holding a single long-stemmed coral rose caught her eye. White linen napkins stood erect between sterling silver flatware, and soft music played in the background.

The waiter came with menus. Gavin opened his and studied it briefly, setting it aside before Carey had read through the entire list of entrees. To her surprise, the restaurant specialized in American cuisine such as prime ribs of beef and boiled lobster.

The waiter returned. "Would you care for something to drink, Carey?" Gavin asked.

"No, thank you, unless, would you mind bringing me a ginger ale?" She sheepishly looked up at the waiter from the corner of her eye.

"Make that two, sir," Gavin added.

The waiter took their order, returning a few minutes later with the ginger ale in exquisite crystal.

"Have you decided what you'd like, Carey?" Gavin asked. "The specialty of the house is prime ribs."

Confused by all the delicious-sounding choices, Carey opted for the easy way out. "That would be fine."

A few minutes later salads appeared, along with freshly ground pepper from a pepper mill added at the table by the waiter.

"Carey," Gavin began thoughtfully, "have you ever wanted to start your own music school?"

Gavin's question surprised and puzzled her. "Why would I want to do that?"

His eyes narrowed on her. "Do you want to go to school all your working life—day in, day out, year after year, teaching the same thing over and over?"

Gavin's questions poured in a torrent over Carey. Her mouth dropped open, and she stared in astonishment. "I happen to like what I'm doing very much, Gavin. Are you putting it down?" Carey defended herself.

Gavin leaned forward, his voice quietly insistent. "Doesn't it bother you, after a year of running your own business, that now you have to follow someone else's rules, live by someone else's schedule?"

Carey put down her fork, her appetite suppressed by the anxious knot twisting inside her stomach. "Gavin, why are you attacking me?"

"I'm not attacking you," he denied urgently.

"Yes, you are. You're mocking my profession, my

livelihood, the occupation I love." Carey's blood ran hotter as she resisted his probing.

"I'm not mocking it," Gavin countered. "I'm merely proposing you consider working for yourself as a music teacher rather than for someone else." His tone softened.

"I like where I work and what I do just fine. What brought all this on, anyway? Can't we please talk about something else?"

Gavin reached for her hand. "Of course we can. I didn't mean to upset you. I just want you to give it some thought. Will you promise me you'll do that?" His eyes searched her expression, filled with a new compassion.

Touched by his tenderness, Carey acquiesced. "Yes. I'll consider it."

Emotionally buffeted by the swing from the carefree happiness of their sightseeing to the searching questions about her occupation, Carey picked at her dinner. Confusion plagued her, and she continued to wonder throughout the meal why Gavin had changed so quickly.

He turned the conversation back to New York, putting forth extra care to smooth the momentary rift, but he never quite succeeded. Carey found it difficult to recapture the closeness she had shared with him formerly.

When they drove out of the city, Carey helped Gavin navigate the routes leading from New York until they reached route 17. Tired from the day's excitement, she dozed on and off until they arrived at Harrington.

Gavin saw her inside, where one dim light burned in the corner of the living room.

"Marilee must still be out with Nick," Carey said, yawning.

"Good," Gavin mumbled, pulling her close with one arm while he shoved the door closed with the other. "Carey, you're not still mad at me, are you?" Small worry lines marred his forehead. "You've been awfully quiet." He held her face in his hands, half whispering.

"I'm just tired, I guess."

Concern melted from his expression, replaced by subtle desire. "Carey, you mean so much to me. I hate to leave you here." Gavin's lips tasted hers, their gentle massage sending currents of warmth through her.

Carey's arms moved instinctively around his neck, her responses to his touch blotting out his earlier harsh words. Lost in her desire to please him, Carey yielded to the intensity of his kiss.

Long moments later, his lips released hers with apparent reluctance. "I have to go before I get carried away with wanting you, Carey," he murmured, "but I'll be back next weekend."

Gavin pulled her in tightly, his strong fingers spread against her back. When her lips left his, she trailed kisses across his jawline, then whispered, "You'd better be back next weekend, or I'll go crazy."

"I'd never let that happen," he promised. Gavin released her, allowing his gaze to travel over her face as if memorizing every feature. Opening the door, he whispered, "Carey, I love you," and was gone.

For several moments, Carey stood motionless. Had she heard Gavin right? Had he told her he loved her? Carey mechanically undressed and dropped into bed, her thoughts floating and swirling over her time with Gavin since his arrival on Friday.

When Monday morning arrived, Carey found herself counting the days until the weekend and her chance to spend more time with Gavin. Even the instrumental lessons requiring her fullest concentration could not completely drive Gavin from her mind.

Gradually, the weekdays faded into the past, and Gavin arrived in Harrington, this time on Saturday. He took her out for an evening of dining and dancing, and attended church with her on Sunday morning.

Throughout October and into November, sharing at least a part of the weekend with each other became their routine. Carey marveled at the loving compassion Gavin displayed toward her, and she reciprocated, wanting nothing more than to spend her time getting to know him better.

Carey loved her students, she enjoyed her job, but slowly came to realize that her life could not be complete without Gavin. In her relationship with Gavin, as in all other areas of her life, Carey sought the Lord's guidance. He seemed to show her that with time, their relationship could grow and endure.

As Thanksgiving time approached, Carey made plans to go to Stockport. Her aunt, uncle, and cousin invited her to share their turkey feast, and Carey looked forward to introducing them to Gavin.

When she let herself into the McIlwain home on Thursday morning, the fragrance of roses surrounded her. She stepped into the center of the living room, and blinked. It was absolutely filled with roses! Red roses, white roses, pink ones, and yellow, covered every flat surface. The television, coffee table, end table, and bookcase all overflowed with Gavin's roses!

She turned toward the dining table, then stepped into the kitchen. More roses! Lavender roses and ivory ones filled the dining room, while tiny peach-colored sweethearts brightened the kitchen. She extracted one white rose from a bouquet and buried her nose in it. Never would she tire of Gavin's roses.

Old memories came flooding back as she carried her

bag to her room at the end of the hall, pausing momentarily outside Todd's room. Her concern for him had never wavered. She wondered what Todd would be thankful for on this special day, whether he had made progress toward curbing his gambling addiction, or had spent hours holding onto a poker hand.

Carey showered and washed her hair. Gavin would accompany her to dinner with her relatives. Leisurely, she dressed in an oyster-white sweater dress, its pattern showing an eyelet design knitted into the bodice. The soft blend of the angora and silk felt comfortably cozy against her skin. Its shape clung gently to her figure, accenting her slim waist.

Carey answered Gavin's knock, a hint of Jean Naté fragrance moving with her.

Gavin pulled her into the warmth of his arms. "You smell great," he breathed against her hair. "I know it's only been a three-day week, but somehow it seemed longer than the others." When his lips met hers, he sent shivers of delight through her.

After a few moments, she pulled back. "I love the roses, Gavin." She kissed his neck. "How did you do it?"

A mischievous look overtook his features. "I have my ways," he answered mysteriously.

"They're waiting on us for dinner," she said with reluctance.

"They'll have to wait a minute longer." Gavin reached into his coat pocket. "Carey, will you marry me?" His eyes pleaded as strongly as his words.

Without a word, Carey placed her mouth over his, showing rather than telling him her answer. Gavin's hands framed her face and held her close. At last, he drew away a bit.

"This will make it official," he explained, popping

open a black velvet ring box to display a dazzling oval solitaire set in yellow gold.

"Gavin," she gasped, "it's indescribably beautiful."

"Not as beautiful as it could be." He removed the ring from its cushion and slipped it onto her finger. Carey didn't know how he had guessed her ring size, and she didn't ask. She only knew that the ring felt right on her finger, just as her relationship with Gavin had come to feel.

Carey enjoyed the opportunity to visit with her relatives during her Thanksgiving dinner. Only one awkward moment occurred when she asked if anyone had heard a word about Todd. Gail and Sue glanced at Gavin, who maintained a sober expression, then they lowered their eyes and said they hadn't heard anything from Todd.

Later that evening, Gavin declined Carey's invitation to come inside. "Business will keep me tied up tomorrow, Carey. Can you manage to fill your day without me?" Gavin caressed her cheek with his fingertip as he spoke.

"I'll manage, though I'll miss you. I want to do some Christmas shopping in Rochester. Looks like tomorrow is the perfect time."

"Let's plan on dinner together tomorrow night. Can you be ready at eight o'clock? I'll take you to the Lincoln Room in Willows Corners, and we'll celebrate our engagement." Gavin's hand moved behind her neck, and Carey reveled in his tender kiss. "And when you're done shopping tomorrow afternoon, you could stop by and say hello to the Emerys. You might be surprised how things have changed."

Though his suggestion made her curious, Gavin disappeared down her driveway before Carey could ask him any questions.

The crowds of Christmas shoppers exhilarated Carey. Bustling throngs milled everywhere and Christmas decorations were already hung throughout all the stores. Santas listened to patiently waiting children tell them of their most earnest Christmas desires.

She returned to Stockport late in the afternoon and stopped by the flower shop. The cold November wind had picked up, causing her to pull her scarf more tightly around her neck.

"Carey, you look absolutely radiant," Maggie beamed, laying red carnations on the arranging table to hug her. "Congratulations! I heard about you and Gavin. I'm so happy for you both."

"Thank you, Maggie, but how could you know already? We've only been engaged since yesterday."

"Word travels fast in this town, Carey. Especially when you're surrounded by relatives." Maggie nodded toward the door separating the retail shop from the first greenhouse.

Carey blinked, then gasped with surprise. "Todd!" She ran to him, hugging him tightly. He hugged her back. "Why haven't you written or called?" Carey demanded, half angry, half relieved.

"My new boss gave me strict orders not to. Gavin said I shouldn't get your hopes up, but Carey, he's seen to it that I get serious about my problem, and now he's helping me buy back the business. Today was my first day on the job." Todd continued his explanation. "For weeks, Gavin has checked my every move, knowing if he didn't, I'd go right back to the poker table. Now that I've developed some self-discipline of my own, he's negotiated a way for me to get the place back from Redgrave, and I'm going to do it, Carey, I know it. Nothing's going to to stop me, as long as God gives me the strength to keep my hands away from a deck of cards."

Carey hugged Todd hard and kissed his cheek, moisture from her eyes dampening his face. "Good for you, little brother. I knew you'd come around in time."

Together, they walked toward the office where Alissa was cleaning out her desk drawers.

"Hello, Carey. Congratulations. I heard." Alissa's smooth low voice purred. She smiled a not ingenuine smile. "Aren't you going to show me the ring?"

Uncomfortable, Carey hesitated. "I didn't think you'd be interested," she explained.

"There are no hard feelings on my part, Carey." Alissa's tone embodied friendly qualities. She reached toward Carey's left hand. Slowly, Carey removed it from her coat pocket and showed Alissa her ring. "It's absolutely stunning, Carey. You must be very happy."

"Thank you, Alissa. I am," Carey answered, baffled by her lack of envy or contempt. Although Alissa's appearance had changed little since Carey last saw her, her attitude was not the same at all.

Floyd approached Carey, having come into the shop from the greenhouse in back. "How's my favorite teacher?" He asked, resting his arm on her shoulder.

"Great," Carey grinned up at him, then pecked him on the cheek.

"I suppose you're spending every available minute with your intended while you're on vacation, then." Floyd winked knowingly.

"Almost every minute," Carey answered. "He was tied up with business all day today." She glanced at the clock. "Now that you mention it, I'd better get home. He's picking me up later for dinner, and I have lots to do before I'm ready."

Floyd chuckled. "Stop by again when you can stay longer."

"Thanks. I'll try."

178

"I'll see you later, Sis," Todd said.

Carey stepped toward Alissa. "Good-by, Alissa."

"Good-by, Carey. Give Gavin my congratulations." Her sultry voice slinked over the words, then she added something under her breath, which almost sounded like, "if you see him." Carey wondered about it for a moment, but decided not to pursue the comment.

Carey hurried home, ecstatic knowing Todd had made a comeback and happily anticipating her date with Gavin. The first snowflakes of the season drifted over her as she walked through the chilling air. Winter clouds loomed overhead, dark and heavy with snow. Gusty blasts of freezing wind licked at her face, and she recalled that the weatherman had predicted the possibility of the first real snowfall of the season occurring tonight.

Carey snuggled into her bathrobe and drew bath water. She slipped into the tub and relaxed. Just like a movie scene, no sooner had her back rested against the end of the tub than the phone began ringing. Carey ignored it, knowing it would stop before she could get out of the tub to answer. Secure in the knowledge that if it were Gavin, he would call back, Carey could think of no one else who might call her.

Ready well before eight, Carey turned on the television and relaxed in the recliner that had been her father's. A small w appeared in the lower left corner of the screen. Carey assumed a snowstorm warning had been issued, and wondered if perhaps she and Gavin should consider staying closer to home for their celebration.

Carey leaned back in the recliner and dozed, then awoke with a start to the sound of the telephone. Her watch said eight-thirty. Gavin was probably calling her back. Carey ran to the phone.

"Hello."

"May I please speak to Gavin Jack?" came the breathy female voice.

"Who is this?" Carey demanded.

"This is a friend of his. I was told I could reach him there," the woman insisted.

"Gavin isn't here. Would you like to leave a message?" Carey asked, thinking she could identify the voice if she heard a little more of it.

"*If* you see him, tell him I'll meet him at the usual time and place on Wednesday." The sultry caller hung up.

At first Carey was stunned by the call. What was the woman talking about? She concentrated again on the caller's voice, and finally she understood. It was Alissa! *So,* Carey thought, *that's why she seemed so friendly. She wanted to set me up for one last dose of her spite.*

"Well," Carey said aloud, "When Gavin gets here we'll both have the last laugh on poor Alissa!"

The scene outside her window interrupted Carey's thoughts. Snow fell thick and fast, illuminated by the the rays of the streetlight. Carey switched on the radio for the latest weather news.

State Police ask that, except in the case of emergencies, you stay off the road tonight. Travel is hazardous as drifts accumulate, closing some roads in the outlying areas. Roads on the north end of the county along the lake are particularly hazardous. Snowplows are not able to keep up with the accumulation.

As interminable minutes dragged by, Carey wondered what reason prevented Gavin from arriving for their date. Had the weather delayed him?

She sorted over and over again the circumstances that

had brought Gavin to her in Harrington to tell her that he cared about her, to tell her that he loved her. He had come on his own. He had taken that bold step at risk of being refused by her.

Worried that something might have happened to Gavin on the road Carey dialed his home phone, but got no answer. She frantically dialed his business number with the same results.

The wind picked up. She could hear it gusting harder against the house. Carey held back the draperies and peered out the front picture window. Drifts had accumulated along the side of the road. The wind blew from the northeast across Lake Ontario and inland to create havoc. Flashbacks of her parents' accident the year before haunted Carey. Would Gavin disappear as suddenly and tragically from her life as they had? Fear clutched her heart; then Carey reminded herself that she could rely on the Lord in all things, and prayed for his safety. Her apprehension lessened a small amount.

Carey thought again about Alissa. Her mind replayed the words, "*If* you see him..." Suddenly another piece of the puzzle snapped into place. Those were the same words she had used this afternoon!

If Alissa would call Carey, might she not also call Gavin, making up some story, sending him off in the wrong direction?

Carey slammed the phone book open on the table and searched for the Redgrave number. She dialed and took a deep breath. Alissa answered.

"Alissa, have you spoken to Gavin tonight?" Carey clipped.

"Carey? Is that you?" she innocently drawled. "I bet you *would* like to know the answer to that, wouldn't you?"

"I *know* Gavin isn't with you, but he's not here either. Did you send him on some wild goose chase?"

"Carey, darling, you'll just have to wait until Gavin comes around, because you aren't getting any information from me. My lips are sealed." She drew out the last word.

"Alissa, do you realize there's a snowstorm moving in off the lake, exactly the kind that killed my parents a year ago? How could you do such a thing as to risk Gavin's life? If anything happens to Gavin, I'll know who to blame—you and your petty jealousy." Carey waited. Silence filled the line. "Good-by, Alissa."

"Carey, wait. I admit I called you earlier this evening, but I haven't spoken to Gavin. If he isn't at your place, it has nothing to do with me." The line went dead.

Carey paced to the front window and peered out again. The drifts were higher. The wind gusted stronger, whipping at the electrical wires. She returned to the phone and dialed Gavin's home. No one answered. Again, she dialed his business, letting the phone ring several minutes. A male voice Carey didn't recognize finally answered.

"Is Gavin Jack there, please? This is Carey McIlwain."

"Gavin's not here. This is Clark. I work for Mr. Jack. We've been trying to batton down the hatches here before the storm does damage to the greenhouses, but he left some time ago for Stockport. Said he had an important date tonight."

"When did he leave, Clark?" Carey panicked.

"Oh, maybe an hour ago."

"Thank you, Clark. If you hear anything from him, will you call me?" She gave him her number, then hung up.

Carey watched the snowplow go by. Heavy chunks of snow landed at the foot of her driveway, closing it off. Even if Gavin made it to her house, he couldn't get into the driveway unless it were shoveled. She wondered whether to go outside and shovel, or wait inside for the phone to ring. After a few minutes of debate, she decided to shovel. It would keep her occupied until he came.

Carey changed into warm outdoor gear, wrapping a double thick mohair scarf around her neck, pulling it up over her nose and mouth. She found the snow shovel in the basement, turned on the outside light, and attacked the accumulation at the foot of her driveway.

Half an hour later, she stopped to phone Clark. He hadn't heard anything from Gavin. Carey's concern increased. Gavin had been headed for Stockport for an hour and a half, and the trip normally took twenty minutes. In his small sports car, he might have slipped off the road, or worse yet, run into another car or truck.

Carey returned to the drive and shoveled faster. If Gavin didn't arrive by the time she finished, she would drive toward Medeena until she found him. Tears crystalized on her cheeks as she thought of finding him in an accident.

Weary from the effort, Carey glanced once at the path she'd cleared. It was wide enough to back her car onto the street, but would be filled again the next time the plow came by. She deposited her shovel on the front porch and grabbed her purse from the house.

Chapter Fifteen

Carey's rusty old Mustang started without hesitation. For once, she was glad she hadn't bothered to buy a new car. At least she wouldn't feel badly if anything happened to this one.

She backed onto the street, and slowly, with her wipers and defroster on high, she drove toward Medeena. As Carey turned down the road heading toward the lake, the snow whipped with more fury, cutting visibility to several feet. Tensely, she gripped the wheel.

Her eyes strained to see through the white sheets of snow whirling in front of her. As she leaned closer to the windshield, her breath clouded her view with condensation. Periodically, she wiped it away with the back of her glove, flexing her fingers, which ached from wrapping so tightly around the steering wheel.

As the car crept slowly toward Medeena, Carey talked to herself and to the Lord, trying to stay calm. She passed several cars that had been abandoned on the side of the road. Flashing lights atop wreckers sent out beacons where motorists were being rescued. Carey continued more cautiously.

Her Mustang's rear end fishtailed, sending shafts of panic into her stomach. Carey's heart pounded in her throat. If she had this much trouble with her Mustang, what had happened to Gavin in his tiny sports car?

Carey approached one particularly open stretch of road. No houses or trees protected it from the increasing wind gusts and snow accumulation. Three-foot-high drifts had closed off her lane entirely, and partially blocked the other.

Hesitantly, Carey proceeded into the other lane. Fortunately, no car lights approached, at least none she could see within the few feet of vibility. Just as she reached the center of the oncoming lane, she felt her tires spinning and the snowdrift clutching her rear wheels.

She panicked. What if she stalled here, in the middle of this barren stretch, with at least a mile between her and the last farmhouse? She couldn't let that happen. She had to find Gavin.

Carey applied pressure to the accelerator. She tried forward, then reverse, again and again, moving a few inches forward each time. Directly ahead, the path widened again to two lanes, if only she could pass through this one bad drift. Carey pressed again on the accelerator and held it down firmly. Her tires whined as they spun. At last, the rear wheels freed themselves from the drift.

A tense sigh of relief escaped her lips, and Carey crept forward on the country road. Faint lights from a car shone through the heavy falling snow. Few people had passed her before her struggle with the last drift, and the next car to encounter it would likely not make it through. As Carey approached the vehicle, she realized that, instead of moving forward, it had slid off the road. She rolled down her window to get a better look.

A man stood next to the small black sports car, waving her down. It was Gavin! Carey's heart leaped for joy at the sight of him. He ran to the side of her car and yanked her door open.

"Carey!" He pulled her into his arms, hugging her so tightly she couldn't breathe.

"Gavin, thank God, you're all right," Carey managed, before his mouth covered hers. Moments later, his lips released hers.

Two hours later, wrapped in a handmade quilt, Carey relaxed on the rug in front of Gavin's roaring fireplace, her head on his shoulder. Their cars, towed safely through the banks of snow, sat in Gavin's circular drive-way. She sipped from the mug of hot cocoa Gavin had prepared for her. Her eyes began to drift shut, her body weary from the physical and emotional strains of the storm.

"Carey, you can't sleep now," Gavin whispered in her ear, then jiggled her.

"I can't seem to keep awake." She spoke through a yawn.

"Carey, look at this," Gavin prodded, reaching for a document on a table an arm's length away. He unrolled a sketch.

Carey sat upright and rubbed her eyes, then focused on the drawing. It was an architect's rendering of an addition.

"Gavin, what is this? Certainly you aren't thinking of expanding this mansion you so quaintly refer to as our future love nest. It's already four times larger than we need." Carey had not been inside Gavin's home until this evening, but Gavin had showed her around briefly after their rescue from the snowstorm. Several bedrooms and baths, plus a spacious living and dining room and an office constituted the main wing of the first and second floors.

186

"I hope you've given some thought by now to working for yourself." Gavin unrolled a second architect's rendering of interior rooms. A larger room marked "music room" was surrounded by several smaller cubicles labeled "lesson rooms."

Puzzled at first, Carey recalled the evening they had dined in New York, and how he had pushed her to become self-employed, versus working for the school system.

"This was the business I had to take care of today," Gavin explained. "I met with the architect, and he presented me with the drawings I'd asked him to prepare following the weekend we went to New York."

"But Gavin," she protested, "this is too much…"

Gavin reached for her hand. "I've been very busy this fall, Carey Jack Brothers Roses is doing better than it ever has before." His eyes searched hers, and his voice took on a hushed, reverent quality, "I was afraid you'd resent me after a while, if you gave up your teaching job to be here with me."

Tears welled in Carey's eyes. She hardly knew what to say, and if she had, the lump in her throat would have made speech difficult. Her lips met his, and she registered her love for him with the sweet urgency of her kiss.

Gavin shared willingly in her affections, responding with an urgency of his own. Moments later, he firmly separated from her and reached for another rolled document, unfurling it before her. "There's more to this project."

It contained cross-section views of all the rooms planned for the music school wing, as well as functional views showing furniture in place and musical equipment including a piano, guitars, chairs, stands, and dozens of musical instruments.

Carey blinked back tears, struggling to find her voice. "Gavin, I love you so much," she managed, her words but a whisper of the emotion she felt for him. "You give me everything I'll ever need for happiness."

Promise Romances™ are available at your local bookstore or may be ordered directly from the publisher by sending $2.25 plus 75¢ (postage and handling) to the publisher for each book ordered.

If you are interested in joining Promise Romance™ Home Subscription Service, please check the appropriate box on the order form. We will be glad to send you more information and a copy of *The Love Letter*, the Promise Romance™ newsletter.

Send to: Etta Wilson
P O Box 141000
Nelson Place at Elm Hill Pike
Nashville, TN 37214-1000

☐ Yes! Please send me the Promise Romance titles I have checked on the back of this page.

I have enclosed _____ to cover the cost of the books ($2.25 each) ordered and 75¢ for postage and handling. Send check or money order. Allow four weeks for delivery.

☐ Yes! I am interested in learning more about the Promise Romance™ Home Subscription Service. Please send me more information and a *free* copy of *The Love Letter*.

Name _____

Address _____

City _____ State _____ Zip _____
Tennessee, California and New York residents, please add applicable sales tax.

OTHER PROMISE ROMANCES YOU WILL ENJOY

$2.25 each

Dear Reader:

I am committed to bringing you the kind of romantic novels you want to read. Please fill out the brief questionnaire below so we will know what you like most in romance.

Mail to: Etta Wilson
Thomas Nelson Publishers
P.O. Box 141000
Nashville, Tenn. 37214

1. Why did you buy this inspirational romance?

   ☐ Author   ☐ Recommendation
   ☐ Back cover description   from others
   ☐ Christian story   ☐ Title
   ☐ Cover art   ☐ Other_____

2. What did you like best about this book?

   ☐ Heroine   ☐ Setting
   ☐ Hero   ☐ Story Line
   ☐ Christian elements   ☐ Secondary characters

3. Where did you buy this book?

   ☐ Christian bookstore   ☐ General bookstore
   ☐ Supermarket   ☐ Book Club
   ☐ Drugstore   ☐ Other (specify)_____

4. Are you interested in buying other Promise Romances™?

   ☐ Very interested   ☐ Somewhat interested
                  ☐ Not interested

5. Please indicate your age group.
   ☐ Under 18   ☐ 25-34
   ☐ 18-24   ☐ 35-49   ☐ Over 50

6. Comments or suggestions?

7. Would you like to receive a free copy of the Promise Romance™ newsletter? If so, please fill in your name and address.

Name _____

Address _____

City _____ State _____ Zip _____

7360-9